D1824376

Beatrix Potter Remembered

Esthwaite Water and the Langdale Pikes (Photo: Aero Pictorial).

Beatrix Potter Remembered

by W. R. Mitchell

Dalesman Books
1987

The Dalesman Publishing Company Ltd
Clapham, Lancaster. LA2 8EB
First published 1987
© W. R. Mitchell, 1987
ISBN: 0 85206 897 2
Printed by Swannack, Brown & Co. Ltd., Hull, England

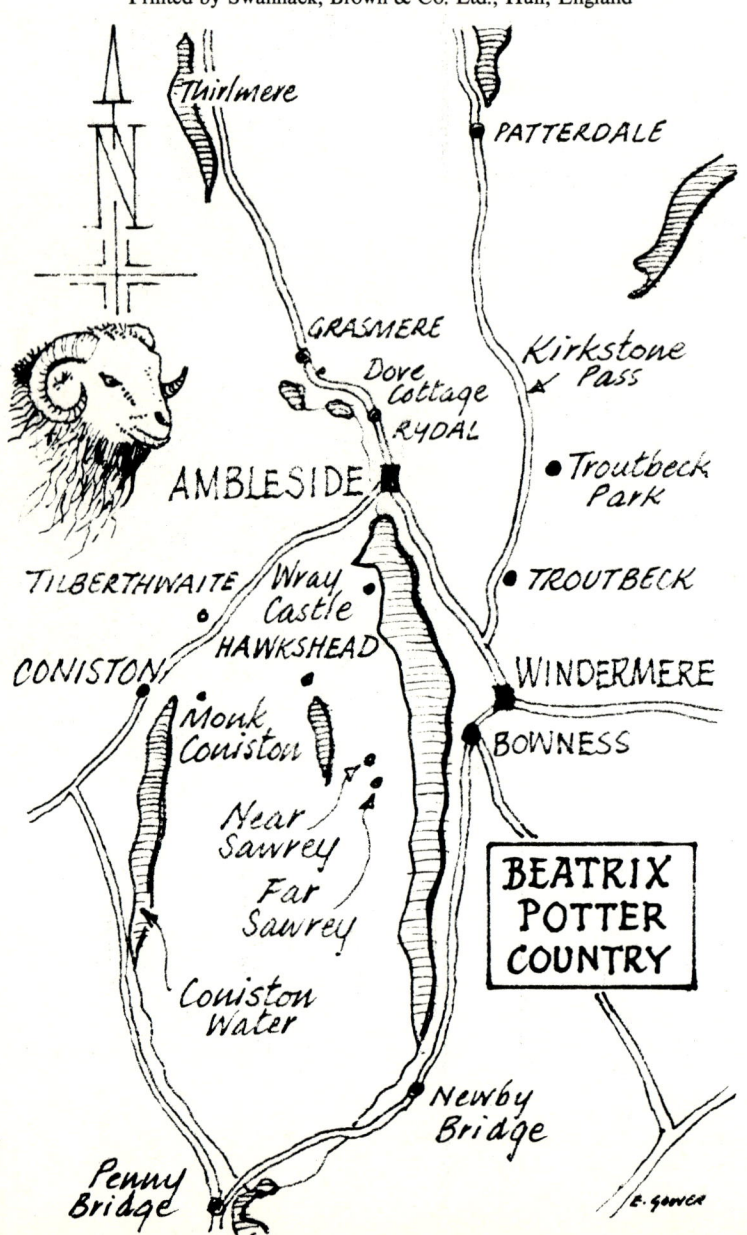

BEATRIX
POTTER
COUNTRY

Contents

Windermere from Brockhole, a sight familiar to Beatrix Potter. At Brockhole lived her cousin, Edith.

Cover photographs:
Front: Beatrix Potter and Kep at Hill Top, Sawrey, 1913 (courtesy of the Victoria and Albert Museum). Hill Top in Centenary Year, 1966 (Photo: F. Leonard Jackson). Anthony Benson, who worked for Beatrix Potter at Troutbeck Park (W. R. Mitchell, who also took all the uncredited photographs in this book). Back Cover: Lambing time at Hill Top Farm.

Above: Lakefield, Sawrey, which the Potters rented for a holiday in the summer of 1896. The house is now called Ees-Wyke. Left: A garden gate at Lakefield which became the subject of a painting by Beatrix Potter.

Foreword

By Mary E. Burkett (Formerly Director of Abbot Hall, Kendal).

BEATRIX POTTER'S NAME bears with it an air of mystery because it is associated with a scientist, a sheep-farmer, an intellectual as well as that of an inspired illustrator and author of children's tales. Many books have been written about her stating emphatically what sort of a person she was. But since then a secret diary has come to light which reveals her as an even more enigmatic figure.

She achieved a style of animal painting which is remarkable not only in its simplicity and purity but in its lack of sentimentality. The animals are, in spite of their clothes, tough little creatures and her awareness of form and action is clearly shown in their obvious character. The lack of pretension and false pomp is clearly illustrated by her indifference to the clothes she wore.

Her popularity, however, increases all the time. When we staged our first exhibition of her work at Abbot Hall, Kendal in February and March 1966, we had more people visiting the gallery then than we had in mid-summer despite the weather. Always people want to know what sort of a person she really was. There are still some people in the Lake District who remember her, and even a few who worked for her. This anthology of people's memories of her will add to the ever-increasing store of information about her. It is an excellent idea of Bill Mitchell, the author, to have accumulated these recollections of 30 or more years of her life and I wish it every success.

An advertisement from about 1949 illustrating the first Beswick Beatrix Potter characters (Photo: courtesy of Royal Doulton, Limited).

Beatrix Potter

Your eyes were always summer.
Common sense, surprise and fun
burnished your internal sun,
lighting your books. Here we find
a cradling-comfort, cats purr
warmth, recognising objects
homely, simple as bee skeps,
tea-pots, feathers, water-butts,
nests with eggs, a fox who struts
sneering, across our dreaming,
first lesson about deceiving.

Clogs on feet, dressed in tweed
conversing with farmers, owt
about sheep, but Herdwicks's breed,
you judged. There can be nowt
worth knowing, you didn't know,
which is why my children's
children stand at my bookshelf
and find their hands go
to Beatrix Potter.

Lydia Thomas

**Sketch for the Frontispiece
to "The Tale of Jemima
Puddle-Duck". Beatrix was
rarely without a sketchbook
when she explored the idyllic
fields and woods overlooking Esthwaite Water.
(Photo: Abbot Hall, Kendal).**

Beatrix Potter and Kep at Hill Top, Sawrey, in 1913 (Photo: Victoria and Albert Museum).

An Introduction

THIS BOOK is based on long conversations with people who knew Beatrix Potter in her later years, when she spent most of her time in the Lake District. The memories are mainly of the last 30 years – the time between her wedding to Willie Heelis, a rather grave Lakeland solicitor, and her death in 1943. Each had reached middle-age when they were married. A man still living in the Sawrey area remembers when Willie was courting. He arrived with motor cycle and sidecar, parking this combination at the end of the drive leading to Hill Top, Beatrix's famous farm. On another day, I heard from Tom Storey, her shepherd, that after her death and cremation, it was he who scattered the ashes at a pre-arranged place not far from the village.

Beatrix Potter is world-famous as the creator of charming little animals with human characteristics. She penned and colourfully illustrated tales that have fascinated generations of children and have also appealed to many grown-ups – tales about Peter Rabbit, Tom Kitten, Jeremy Fisher, Jemima Puddleduck and the other engaging characters whose lives were spent against a backdrop of the meres and fells of the Lake District. That was the public side of Beatrix Potter. She also had an intensely private aspect of her life and would doubtless have been embarrassed had she known that many personal details of that life would in due course be published. She kept a journal in code. That code was "cracked" by Leslie Linder and suddenly we were aware of her life in fine detail between the ages of 15 and 30.

She who craved affection as a child led a secluded and lonely childhood in a straight-laced upper middle class home. The shy young woman, thrown back largely on her own resources, developed a considerable range of interests, including natural history and art. She revelled in the long summer holidays in Scotland and the Lake District and she benefited from the company of distinguished and kindly friends of the family. In later life, she wore cloth made from the wool of her beloved Herdwick sheep, and she clattered around in clogs, which kept her feet firm and dry. Now she was Mrs. Heelis, farmer and landowner, finding special pleasure at agricultural shows and in the company of the elite of Lakeland flockmasters.

Beatrix Potter Remembered, which tells of her later years, has been in my mind for over 30 years, since a chance remark – "I remember Beatrix Potter" – by Mrs. Richards, the former Miss Annie Black of Sawrey, recalled the real Beatrix and not the romanticised figure. I heard of the famous author and illustrator and landowner as one who trudged through the quiet village of Sawrey with rounded shoulders, silky white hair and a face that remained fresh-looking, even cherubic. Beatrix had brilliant blue eyes. Mrs. Richards, who well remembered the clothes of homespun Herdwick wool, added some minor details – two huge patch pockets at the sides and an old straw hat held firmly to her head by black tape tied under her chin. Her dress came down to her ankles, revealing an inch or two of worsted stockings. These stockings were "a kind of heather mixture".

What surprised me, as I conversed with Mrs. Richards, was the fact that local children feared her, probably because she looked so strange. Young people flattened themselves against the walls as she went by and, when she had passed, they ran away as fast as they could. Local people tended to regard her as eccentric, distrusting the way she kept her affairs to herself and tut-tutting over her choice of attire.

In 1955, when I made my first special excursion to the Beatrix Potter Country to chat with those who knew her, there was a romance about the Lake District which no longer exists. A high proportion of native folk occupied the quiet little villages. The roads appeared to have only just outgrown their old status as country lanes and they carried very little traffic. In those days before the farming revolution, which led to much ploughing and re-seeding and a tediously green landscape, there were fields of flowers. Beatrix lived at a time when the pace of life was slow and when people were contented, whatever their means. Some families were very poor.

Those long years ago, I crossed Windermere on what was then a new ferryboat, *Drake*, and trudged up Ferry Hill, entering an area of rounded hills rather than of craggy mountains; of woods, reed-fringed lakes and tarns; of field walls made without mortar and farmhouse walls liberally white-washed. Beatrix's watercolours fix Sawrey and its district as it was in calmer times. She kept herself busy, judging sheep at agricultural shows and sitting on committees. One group was concerned with the preservation of footpaths. She and Willie Heelis did not flaunt their wealth; they lived simply, invariably going their own ways, not getting under each other's feet. Margaret Lane wrote in *A Tale of Beatrix Potter* of "law books and papers and deed-boxes at one end of the dining-room, bramble jelly and toasted teacakes at the other. There were no tiresome concessions to appearance."

To hear first-hand accounts of this remarkable woman has been, for me, a joyful experience. Mrs. Richards may have been frightened of her as a child and she certainly thought of Beatrix as being strange, but respected her for what happened on the day Mrs. Richards' father, Dick Black, died. Beatrix arrived at the house and asked if she could see him. "I took her upstairs; when I turned the sheet back from my dead father's face, she knelt down and wept. 'I've always respected you,' she said. 'God bless you.' I was never so near to tears."

Low Yewdale, a farm on the Monk Coniston estate, which Beatrix Potter bought in 1930. This farm has a splendid "spinning gallery".

I am indebted to Mary Burkett for a memory of Beatrix concerned with hunting. Peter Gaddum, who was related to her through marriage, was keen on field sports, an interest which Beatrix most certainly did not share. "She took great delight in being sarcastic. Telephoning him one Sunday, she said: 'Peter, I think you had better go and look for your dogs. I think they're rabbiting on the Tongue' (at Troutbeck Park)." This was a great insult to a fox-hunter. In later years, Mrs. Gaddum, who lived at Braban House, Burneside, told Mary Burkett that Beatrix had a dry sense of humour. She was also by nature a retiring person. "She did not like people coming up to her, fussing, asking for her autograph and saying nice things about her books."

Beatrix was a spirited person. Dr. J. N. Warren recalled for me when his family lived on the eastern shore of Windermere directly opposite Sawrey. "About twice a week Miss Potter would row across and moor her boat at our little pier, then walk the two and a half miles to Bowness for shopping. I was then about six years old and I remember her as a dowdily dressed, kindly lady with a weather-beaten complexion. She took a fancy to my young brother and would often stop to chat to him in his pram. One day she presented him with some beautifully embroidered 'Peter Rabbit' slippers, fashioned by her own hands. Miss Potter subsequently married Mr. Heelis, an Ambleside solicitor, whose nephew went to my school. One Sunday, I was his guest at the country house of the 'formidable' Colonel Potter. (When the Colonel let us boys loose in his strawberry bed, I reckoned the epithet most unjustified!). What a pity those slippers were not preserved!"

I first met Tom Storey in 1955. He had arrived at Sawrey from Troutbeck, some 60 years ago. Beatrix's days as writer and artist were by no means over, and she gave him the first copy of her *Fairy Caravan*. She told him of a desire to paint a lamb and asked Tom to let her have the head of the next lamb to die. Tom did so. She fastened the head against a wall and sat on a copy (stool) in a field to paint it! I recall with special clarity

They Remember
Beatrix Potter

Right: Amanda Thistlethwaite, nee Postlethwaite, a native of Sawrey, who regularly met Beatrix Potter. **Below, left:** Josephina Banner who, with her husband Delmar, visited Castle Cottage, the home of Beatrix Potter, and also met her at Eskdale Show. **Below, right:** Anthony Benson, who was a shepherd at Troutbeck Park.

my last meeting with Tom. Arriving at his cottage home in Sawrey, I rapped my knuckles against the door and listened for his ever-bright "Come in". This time, the response was delayed. There was time to glance through the window, and to notice that his favourite chair was empty, before I heard his voice faintly inviting me to enter. Tom lay in bed, suffering from an old chest complaint. A few weeks before, he had told me of his impending 90th birthday. I asked him about it. "It's today," he announced. We celebrated, Tom and I, with glasses of sherry. We chatted for a while until members of his devoted family arrived with gifts and good wishes.

Anthony Benson, who lives at Plumpton Foot, a quiet area not far from Penrith, was for 15 years the shepherd at Troutbeck Park. He got to know Beatrix well. Anthony left Troutbeck when his daughter's schooldays were over, being concerned about the difficulty she might have in travelling from the remote farm to a place of work. He told me, with mock gravity, that in 15 years Beatrix had not paid him once. A pause, and he added: "She usually paid t'wife, saying that money should go into the home!"

Mrs. Amanda Thistlethwaite, born at Sawrey but for many years a resident of Hawkshead, told me about Beatrix and allowed me to copy some photographs, two of which had been 'taken' by Beatrix herself. One is a study of Mrs. Thistlethwaite's mother and members of her family, who were posing beside a tree at Ees-Wyke, Sawrey. Another photograph was the basis of a water-colour in a Beatrix Potter book. Mr. Postlethwaite was nicknamed "Possie" by Beatrix, to the annoyance of his wife. The Postlethwaites lived near Castle Cottage and so they saw each other almost daily. He was reticent about being photographed, so he turned his back to the camera. Beatrix photographed the back view, and used it in her picture to great effect.

Children undoubtedly found the elderly Beatrix very strange, but Willow Taylor of Sawrey told me that if you were able to converse with her at her level, she was at ease with you. "Once, when I was in my teens at Kelsick School, Ambleside I wanted to borrow a spinning wheel. We were staging scenes from *Cranford*. I called at Castle Cottage and was invited inside. She sat in her favourite rocking chair and wanted to know all about school. And she was only too willing to lend me the spinning wheel for the play."

* * *

Special thanks are extended to these past or present residents of the Lake District for help received during the compilation of this book: Josephina Banner, Anthony Benson, Mrs. Frank Birkett, Charlie Brown, Mary Burkett, Annie Richards, Tom Storey (who died in March, 1986, at the grand old age of 90), Willow Taylor, Amanda Thistlethwaite, William Waddington, Dr. J. N. Warren, C. T. Williamson, and the staff of The National Trust.

Through the Years

Old jetty at Brockhole, by Windermere lake.

1863 (August 8): Rupert Potter, aged 31, marries Helen Leech, aged 24, in the Unitarian chapel at Hyde, near Manchester.

1866 (July 28): Birth of Helen Beatrix at No. 2 Bolton Gardens, London.

1869: Rupert Potter is elected a member of the Photographic Society of London.

1871: Rupert leases Dalguise House, near Dunkeld, for a summer holiday. Young Beatrix is fascinated by the rich and varied wildlife of the district. (Her childhood nurse, a native of the Highlands, had spoken excitedly about witches and fairies!).

1872: Birth of Bertram, a brother for Beatrix.

1882: Mr. and Mrs. Rupert Potter, discovering that Dalguise House in Scotland is unavailable this year, rent Wray Castle, a Victorian folly overlooking Windermere, for a long holiday. Rupert photographs the castle's stern exterior, and Beatrix (aged 16) spends part of the holiday producing water-colours, including a study of a delightfully overcrowded library. Family outings include some boating on Windermere.

1885: The Potters stay at Larkfield Villa, Ambleside. (They are driven up Great Langdale. Beatrix, now a dark and alert little beauty, with hair swept back and dresses at ankle length, is much impressed by Dungeon Ghyll).

1886: A holiday in the Ambleside district is based on the *Low Wood Hotel*. ("Do not care for the Peaks, a poor starved country, extraordinary number of dead sheep").

1887 (September): The Potters are at Lingholm, overlooking Derwentwater and Skiddaw. (About this time, Beatrix was suffering from the effects of rheumatic fever. Ill health had affected her badly in the spring, when she had been taken to Grange-over-Sands).

1889: The Potters tarry at Holehird, Windermere. Beatrix receives instruction in the skills of driving a pony carriage; she finds much pleasure in touring the country lanes.

1891: Beatrix submits material, including sketches, to the publishers of children's books. Included in the list is Frederick Warne, who expresses interest in an idea for a book.

1892 and 1893: The Potters spend their summer holidays in Scotland. (Beatrix begins to form a good collection of fossils collected in Scotland and Lakeland).

1895 (August): A return to Holehird for a holiday. (On an excursion, Beatrix is "very much struck with the ideal beauty of Coniston . . . in my opinion far the most beautiful of the larger Lakes"). In this year, Canon Rawnsley (with Miss Octavia Hill and Sir Robert Hunter) form a National Trust. Rupert Potter becomes the first Life Member. (Rawnsley, a great friend of the Potters, is a classical scholar, an admirer of Ruskin and a man who writes copiously about Lakeland life and affairs. His wife, Edith, is a keen amateur artist. She recognises Beatrix's talent as a water-colourist).

1896: The Potters rent Lakefield, Sawrey, for a summer holiday. (The house is now called Ees-Wyke).

1899: Hardwicke Rawnsley establishes the Herdwick Sheepbreeders' Association.

1901: Publication of *The Tale of Peter Rabbit* (black and white edition of 250 copies, printed privately). In this year died Peter, Beatrix's pet rabbit, "at the end of his 9th year."

1902: Frederick Warne publish *The Tale of Peter Rabbit*. ("It was written to a child – not made to order."). *The Tailor of Gloucester* is printed privately (edition of 500 copies).

1903: The Potters spend their summer holiday at Fawe Park, Derwentwater. *The Tale of Squirrel Nutkin* and *The Tailor of Gloucester* (re-issued by Warnes).

1904: Appearance of *The Tale of Benjamin Bunny* and *The Tale of Two Bad Mice*.

1905: Beatrix is engaged to Norman Dalziel Warne, of the publishing family. A shy man, his formal proposal is by letter. Beatrix's parents are displeased at the prospect of her marrying "into the trade". (Norman dies suddenly, on August 25, of pernicious anaemia, aged 37).

1905: Beatrix buys Hill Top, Sawrey. (She becomes, in spirit at least, a farmer, as her brother Bertram had done some years before). Appearance of *The Tale of Mrs. Tiggy-Winkle* and *The Pie and the Patty-pan*.

1906: Hill Top, Sawrey, is extended to house Beatrix's farm manager. Publication of *The Tale of Mr. Jeremy Fisher*.

1907: *The Tale of Tom Kitten* (a book in Sawrey, with views of Hill Top and its garden).

1908: *The Tale of Jemima Puddle-duck* (written for Ralph and Betsy, the children of John Cannon, manager of Hill Top Farm) and *The Tale of Samuel Whiskers* (written about 1905 and set at Hill Top).

1909: Beatrix buys Castle Farm at Sawrey (converts the farmhouse, adds the fields to Hill Top, and buys Moss Eccles tarn, planting it with water lilies and stocking it with fish). *The Tale of Flopsy Bunnies* (set in Wales) and *Ginger and Pickles*. Hardwicke Rawnsley becomes a Canon of Carlisle.

1910: Beatrix campaigns vigorously for tariff reform in the period before a general election. To her dismay, the Liberal Government is returned. *The Tale of Mrs. Tittlemouse* appears.

1911: Publication of *The Tale of Timmy Tiptoes* and *Peter Rabbit's Painting Book*.

1912: Beatrix is shocked when a flying boat touches down on the once quiet Windermere. She describes the machine as "a beastly, fly-swimming spluttering aircraft".

1913: *(October)*. Beatrix is married to William Heelis at St. Mary Abbot's in

Experts on Lakeland sheep. The third from the left is Tom Storey, who for many years worked for Beatrix Potter at Hill Top, Sawrey.

18

Kensington, London. (The honeymoon is spent at Sawrey). Publication of *The Tale of Pigling Bland*.

1914: Beatrix makes a number of journeys to London because her father is seriously ill. (Rupert Potter dies on May 8).

1919: Beatrix's widowed mother settles at Lindeth How, Storrs, along with four maids, two gardeners and the coachman who is now the chauffeur. Beatrix is among those who endow a charity to maintain a district nurse in the parishes of Sawrey, Hawkshead and Wray.

1920: Death of Canon Rawnsley. (He had a considerable influence on Beatrix, to the extent that she became one of the early supporters of the National Trust and was to leave 4,000 acres and property to the Trust).

1923: Beatrix buys Troutbeck Park, a large fell farm. (She is very fond of this place. "There is a largeness and silence going up into the hills"). A Morris Cowley vehicle, driven by Walter, who had been her mother's footman, enables her to visit Troutbeck Park at regular intervals.

1926: Beatrix appoints Tom Storey as her shepherd. (It is in this year that the title *The Roly-Poly Pudding* is changed to *The Tale of Samuel Whiskers*).

1929: *The Fairy Caravan* is published in America.

1930: Beatrix buys the large Monk Coniston Estate, which includes Tarn Hows, Tom Heights, Tilberthwaite, Yewdale and the summit of Wetherlam. Beatrix becomes the first woman president of the Herdwick Sheepbreeders' Association. At show time, she sometimes refers to her prize-winning Herdwicks as "our pretty little Baas". (This is a time of industrial depression and much urban unemployment. Prices for sheep taken to the autumn sales are poor. And at Hill Top, the summer's wool clip was slow to find a buyer).

1932 (December 20): Death of Helen Potter, the mother of Beatrix. Attending to her in her later years has been quite a trial for Beatrix, but she is not often heard to complain.

1939: Beatrix has a breakdown in health and spends a little time in hospital.

1939-42: Beatrix welcomes to Sawrey her cousin, Sir William Hyde Parker, of Melford Hall. He, his Danish wife Ella and their children, rendered homeless because of war conditions, are allowed to live in Hill Top. (Sir William, a great angler, soon joins Willie Heelis at Moss Eccles Tarn). During the war, the original drawings for all Beatrix's books are kept at Sawrey rather than in war-torn London. The American interest in her work continues to astound Beatrix. She continues to provide a camping ground at Sawrey for Girl Guides and enjoys their visits. In 1940, No 2 Bolton Gardens, Beatrix's "unloved birthplace", is destroyed by bombs.

1943 (July 27): Girl Guides, in camp at Sawrey dress up as characters from Beatrix's books and appear before her at Castle Cottage on her 77th birthday. (*December 22*). Death of Beatrix, quietly, at her Sawrey home. Cremation at Blackpool. The death notice contains these requests: "No mourning, no flowers and no letters, please."

1946: Hill Top, Sawrey, is opened to the public by The National Trust.

1966: Leslie Linder publishes his transcript of the journal of Beatrix Potter.

1970: Mr. Linder gives near 300 Potter drawings and paintings to the National Book League.

1973: Leslie Linder and Enid, his sister, leave over 2,000 items of Beatrix Potter interest to the Victoria and Albert Musuem as part of the National Art Library.

1979: The Post Office, in the International Year of the Child, issues four stamps, one of which features three Beatrix Potter characters – Peter Rabbit, Jemima Puddle-duck and Squirrel Nutkin.

1980: Founding of The Beatrix Potter Society, which seeks to promote the study and appreciation of her life and works.

A Sparkle on Windermere.

Top: Brockhole in winter (Photo: Geoffrey Berry). Above: The Mansion as it neared completion. Right: Edith Gaddum (Photos: Courtesy of Brockhole, the National Park Centre).

Above: Sawrey, where Beatrix Potter spent her later years. Below: A view across one of her meadows to Castle Cottage, where she actually lived, Hill Top being a repository for many well-loved objects and a place to be regularly visited.

At Home in Sawrey

ONLY AFTER her marriage in 1913 did Beatrix live full-time at Sawrey, a place she had known – and loved – since the Potters rented a summer holiday home overlooking Esthwaite Water. Looking back on her early visits, she wrote of Sawrey: "It is as nearly perfect a little place as I ever lived in and such nice old-fashioned people in the village." On another occasion she recalled the "very pretty hill country, but not wild like Keswick or Ullswater."

There are two Sawreys, Near and Far. They were named after their positions in relation to Hawkshead, which had been a bustling place for centuries. The old road to Kendal passed Esthwaite Water and traversed the two little villages on its way to the ferry crossing at Windermere. At Near Sawrey, the splendid house now known as Ees-Wyke comes into view. The Potters came here for a long stay in 1896 and Beatrix painted some of its features, also an old oak tree in the field sloping down to the lake.

Josephina Banner relates that Beatrix toured the Lake District in "an antiquated, strange-looking black car, very much like a taxi, and driven by a very ancient chauffeur." When attending outdoor events she often carried an umbrella which had belonged to Mr. Warne, a partner in the publishing firm, to whom she might have been married but for his untimely death. Beatrix, a Unitarian, was not known to attend the parish church at Sawrey. She did frequent the Quaker Meeting House at Colthouse from time to time and, having arranged to visit her mother, when she lived at Lindeth Howe, Beatrix would continue to go to Church at Troutbeck.

Sawrey was a quiet area. Within living memory, children used the main road as a playground. "We played rounders there," recalls Mrs. Amanda Thistlethwaite, of Hawkshead, who – as a child, Amanda Postlethwaite – regularly met and had brief chats with Beatrix Potter. "Sawrey was a lovely unspoilt little village then."

The Postlethwaites of High Green Gate were near neighbours of the Heelis family of Castle Cottage. So close were the two houses that there could be territorial disputes. The geese belonging to the Postlethwaites found their way into Beatrix's garden and began to crop the lawn. "Mrs. Heelis came to the door and said to my mother: 'Will you tell Possie – that was her name for my father, and mother didn't care to hear it – to get his geese off my land. They're eating all my grass.' She was very bitter about anything like that."

About a fortnight later, Beatrix's turkeys were on the Postlethwaite's land. "Now my mother was one of the sweetest women you could ever wish to meet. (She used to tell my father to stop arguing with Beatrix, for they often discussed farming and he knew he was wrong. He argued simply to make her annoyed). When the turkeys were on our land, my mother saw red, for hadn't Beatrix told her off about our geese? Mother walked across to Castle Cottage, went up their drive and knocked at the door. When it had been opened, mother said: 'Mrs. Heelis, will you take your turkeys off our land? You wouldn't allow our geese to be on yours'. It wasn't a bit like mother to do this, but the incident of the geese still rankled with her."

At Castle Cottage, two widows – Mrs. Benson and Mrs. Rogerson – did the housework and the cooking. They did not "live in", having cottages in the village. Tommy Christopherson attended to the garden, Tommy Willan was the handy man and a small orchard at the back of the house was left to look after itself. Tom Storey, who called daily with milk, told me: "Mrs. Heelis was always up and about in good time. You'd hear the clatter of her clogs on the flagged floors." Anthony Benson, when visiting Castle Cottage, got no further than a chair just inside the kitchen. "That's where you sat, about two paces in. She'd fetch you a cup o'tea, and one meat sandwich, and that was that!" Anthony usually called on his way back to Troutbeck Farm, after attending to sheep on her other farms. "She would never say: 'I'll take you back'. After your cup o'tea, you'd to walk down to t'ferry, cross Windermere and tramp up Bowness and on to Troutbeck." Anthony added: "There wasn't a day long enough."

Josephina recalls her first visit to this house, and the way that she and her husband had to go through the gardens of two other houses to reach it. (Later, they became acquainted with a back door which gave access to the back lane). Beatrix cherished the obscurity of her residence, not because she disliked people but simply because fame ensured a regular flow of visitors. If she were to be well-disposed to them all, no time would be left for leisure or other interests.

On the first visit to Castle Cottage, Josephina had to rap her knuckles on the small green door, there being no knocker to use. "There was a long silence. Then Delmar and I heard little clogs toddling along on the flags beyond the door. They toddled up to the door. Then they stopped. We felt it was just like a little mouse, stopping to sniff the air, to try and detect who was coming. Then gradually she opened the door until it was two or three inches wide. We saw her little face peep through. She recognised us. She opened the door a little and said: 'Come in.' And do you know what she was wearing on her head? One of those old-fashioned tea-cosies which are knitted and have a hole for the spout!" It is recalled that the tea-cosy was blue. "She looked so cute with it on." Beatrix did not shake hands with her visitors. "She turned and toddled off. We just followed her. Delmar shut the door behind us. We found ourselves in a flagged hall. There was no mat. Two beautiful old guns, with silver mountings, adorned a beam. Then, on the right, there was a door into this lovely old room."

Three photographs of High Green Gate, Sawrey. Above, left: Mary Postlethwaite making bread. Above, right: Mrs. Postlethwaite and daughter framed by the wooden porch in which Mr. Postlethwaite and Beatrix Potter (a close neighbour) used to sit and discuss farming. Below: A general view of the farmhouse and the porch (Photos: Collection of Amanda Thistlethwaite).

It was not over-furnished. There was a fireplace, with two easy chairs, with red velvet. I remember an old-fashioned dining table. "We saw some chocolate wrappers – what Delmar later declared was 'a naughty amount of chocolate paper'. Some straight-backed chairs were available, and the visitors sat on these. We sat here, rather politely, because Beatrix was very awe-inspiring as well as being sweetly pretty." She began to ask questions. "As we answered, and she discovered that we knew the Lakes intimately, she began to open up and became very friendly. She said something very funny: I laughed, and as I laughed I snorted. My husband said: 'Oh, Pig-wig', a nickname that made Beatrix laugh. She very often use this name when she wrote to me."

Josephina has such a clear recollection of that first visit to Castle Cottage that she can recall fine details of a Girton painting that hung there. "It was so suitable – a shepherd, sheep and an approaching storm." At the time the Banners became acquainted with Beatrix, she no longer had the keenness of sight to enable her to paint delicate water-colours. She cherished her original paintings, each measuring about 12 by 8 inches. Wrapped in brown paper, with a blue ribbon, they were left behind the geyser in the bathroom at Castle Cottage. "Even in this matter, she was completely original."

Amanda Thistlethwaite recalls the austere appearance of rooms at Castle Cottage. In the kitchen, there was nothing smart, "just bare flags, a scrubbed table and ordinary ladder-backed chairs. Yet, everything was beautiful and clean. hams were hanging in the pantry." From the kitchen, a visitor could walk down a passage into what was called the lounge. "I don't think she had a fitted carpet, just a carpet in the middle of the room, as people did in those days." Mrs. Thistlethwaite recalls a piano, a settee and some easy chairs. One or two small tables stood about. From the lounge one might go on to a kind of verandah. "It looked on to the garden. She had an extension, for a big bedroom, made; it had lovely bay windows."

My own first insight into what life was like at Sawrey at the time Beatrix lived there was the conversation I had over 30 years ago with Annie Richards (nee Black). Her parents were well-known residents of the village who eventually moved into a cottage standing in Beatrix Potter's farmyard. The Black family now saw more of Beatrix than they had done before and they began to know her true self. "Behind that quaint dress and bent head there was a very beautiful character. Even my father began to think there was 'nowt much wrang' with her after all. Her many kindnesses she showed towards my parents are too numerous to mention, but this I must tell you . ." She recalled how there was an orchard adjoining the farmyard. It was well stocked with apples and plum trees. Beatrix Potter came to the cottage of the Black family and said: "Now there are my fruit trees. I don't want you to help yourselves, but I have given you one apple and one plum tree. I've put a red band round each of them. You can have the fruit from those two trees." As Annie pondered about that incident, she saw behind it a great moral. "Beatrix Potter must have thought all that fruit would be a temptation, so to avoid it she offered some of it to the children. It was much nicer to have a tree to pick from than to be given a basketful of fruit."

William H. Waddington, a well-known Lakeland artist, lived close enough to Beatrix to be able to see her almost every day. In 1916, and for some years afterwards, the Waddingtons occupied one of her properties. In 1959, he told me: "When I first approached Beatrix about accommodation, we were received in a most kindly way. 'I think I would rather like to have an artist living next door,' Beatrix had said. 'He would not have a gramophone going in the garden . . .' " She began to enumerate many other things which she did not believe a self-respecting artist would do. "I'm quite sure that you, as an artist, would agree with me," she concluded. Mr Waddington replied: "As a matter of fact, where I have been I could have wished to have seen far less of my landlord, so this will suit me very well."

The Friends Meeting House at Colthouse. A Unitarian, Beatrix Potter occasionally worshipped with the Quakers. She was driven to Colthouse in a horse-drawn carriage.

A person of very regular ways, Beatrix passed along the drive at the bottom of the Waddington's garden every morning at precisely the same time – followed by turkeys, ducks, geese and any other feathered creatures that happened to be near. These were attracted by the hot mash she carried in a bucket. Beatrix had a stick with which she stirred the mash. She beat the bucket and all the time she sang a cadence of song.

What was Beatrix Potter like as a landlord? "She could not have been kinder," said Mr. Waddington. "She made me a big studio in the house by arranging for a wall to be knocked down; she went to considerable expense to make it a comfortable home." Beatrix did not care much for change. Old Mrs. Black painted the door of the cottage dark green but, impulsively, decided that two panels should be white. Beatrix was soon on the doorstep demanding that the decoration of the door should be a uniform green. Mrs. Thistlethwaite confirms her dislike of novelty and says that after she and her husband were married, they had a wireless pole erected to improve the reception. "And do you know, we only had it up two days when Mrs. Heelis, she came up those steps and said to me: 'Amanda, who gave you permission to put that wireless pole up?' I said: 'Our landlord', which was Bob Taylor. I said to her: 'You only have to ask your landlord, surely.' Beatrix snapped: 'Well, it's to come down. You can tell Robert he's to take it down.' I said: 'Very well, I'll tell my husband when he comes'." Robert wrote her a letter, which she never answered. "Bob told her that he had had permission to put the aerial up. If she wanted it taken down, she must find the labour. The workmen must – it was silly really! – dig it out and take it from the bottom!" The Thistlethwaites, thinking about the incident, realised it was a dreadful pole. "It was in the days when you thought the higher the pole went, the better was the radio reception."

After leaving school, Mrs. Thistlethwaite worked on her father's farm for two years – a farm standing close to Castle Cottage. There were lots of encounters with the redoubtable Beatrix. "I used to clean the shippons out, and if she came out of her back gate she would pass the time of day and say: 'Are you working again, Amanda?' Or something like that." Mrs. Thistlethwaite had milked cows from being nine years old till she was 19. "We had 10 cows, though I wouldn't milk 10 at any one time. We had pigs and sheep – Herdwicks and Swaledales."

Amanda then went to work at the small grocer's shop owned by the Taylors. "I worked here for four years. People only bought Jack-o'-the-Pinch (when they'd run out of anything!), and so the little shop had to close. Beatrix wrote about this little shop in *Ginger and Pickles*. In her day, the windows had small panes. You went down this passage and in at the right hand side, and then it had a counter and it wasn't much bigger then the living room of a house. We kept our flour in an oak chest. Herbs and spices were kept in small wooden drawers. It was a lovely little shop. You'd see bacon hanging up and we had to cut lard to demand . . ." Beatrix was a regular customer. "I served her many a time. She'd come probably for some sugar, if she'd run short, or for some sweets." When Amanda was to be married and leave the shop, Beatrix came to the door and announced: "Mr. Heelis says I've got to give you a present."

A photograph of Mr. Postlethwaite, farmer of Sawrey, taken by Beatrix Potter. He did not wish to be photographed and had turned away. Beatrix took a study of his back, and used the picture as the basis of a water-colour in one of her books! Look carefully and you will see there are two of his children on the picture. One stands immediately behind the other (Photo: Courtesy of Amanda Thistlethwaite).

Mrs. Chapman, a Sawrey character, the wife of a woodman, would be well known to Beatrix Potter, who passed her home on most days of the week. In her later life, Mrs Chapman sported a bushy beard! (Photo: Collection of Amanda Thistlethwaite).

In the quiet and restful air of the *Tower Bank Arms*, at Sawrey, 30 years ago, Mrs. Margaret Burns told me her recollections of Beatrix Potter. "I saw her every day. We often chatted under an old apple tree. There's no two ways about it – she was a character. I liked her very much but, mind you, if anyone got on the wrong side of her I don't think they ever got back into her favour again. I used to either say nothing or side with her. It was the best way. She was a most interesting lady. You could talk to Beatrix Potter and be sure that what she said would be very interesting. As far as children were concerned, she used to be very good to them – if they behaved themselves. Lots of people thought her hard. I have never thought so. I think she was good." One night there was a sing-song in the *Tower Bank Arms*, when Lakeland hunting songs were being rendered by the village folk to celebrate a John Peel anniversary. Beatrix Potter would not come into the building, but she paced up and down outside, listening to the music.

The "Tower Bank Arms" at Sawrey. This hostelry, which stands near Hill Top, was kept by William and Margaret Burns in the days of Beatrix Potter. The Burns family held the licence for 35 years. Beatrix was recalled as being "very sweet on some occasions, austere at other times..."

Willow Taylor, the daughter of Mrs. Burns, says that Beatrix came into the hotel "only when she wanted to tell my father that I'd been a naughty girl! She was very friendly with my mother and had long conversations with her. She was always having to complain about me climbing walls . . ." Willow recalls that Girl Guides camped at Bull Banks, which was on Beatrix's land. "She liked the Guides and she visited them. They used to walk across to the barn and fill their palliases with hay. At the end of the day, we all joined them round a camp fire and drank cocoa."

Mrs. Dorothy Harrison, of Kendal, recalls that her mother-in-law had a friend, a Mrs. Wright, who lived next door to Beatrix at Sawrey. "I understand that the cat used in Beatrix Potter's stories belonged to Mrs. Wright." Marjorie Huddleston, now living at Portsmouth, recalls days spent at Skelwith Bridge, where her father was head teacher at the school. "My mother was on a committee for something to do with hospitals and used to go to Brathay for meetings. I once met Beatrix Potter there. She was also on the committee. I knew her husband, Mr. Heelis, and I once danced with him at a folk dance party held in Hawkshead."

Mr. Postlethwaite and Beatrix, who were close neighbours at Sawrey, would sit in the porch at High Green Gate and talk for hours about sheep. Amanda, his daughter, recalls: "After a while, my father would get up in his majesty, and Beatrix would get up in her majesty, and she'd remark: 'You're not worth talking to Possie.' He'd retort: 'No more are you, Mrs Heelis.' She'd say: 'You'd better get yourself on to t'fell where you've nobody to fall out with – that's your best place.' Yet, next day, Beatrix Potter was back, talking to him. She never bore any malice."

Springtime at Hill Top, Sawrey.

Beatrix Potter's water-colour of "Mrs. Rabbit & Son, Greengrocer", with doors, shutters and basket-lids that open to reveal members of the Rabbit family and the greengrocer's produce (Photo: Courtesy of Sotheby's).

Hill Top, Sawrey (National Trust).

34

Treasures at Hill Top

HILL TOP, at Sawrey, was a place to which Beatrix resorted for some of her quiet pursuits, such as painting, and it was here that many of her treasures were stored. Josephina Banner recalls the rabbit kept in a hutch in the garden, "so that children would not be too disappointed if they visited the place and could not find Peter Rabbit." The hutch was of the bottomless type that could be moved to fresh grazing land daily. Its inmates were introduced to children as being "relations of Peter Rabbit." Josephina adds that Beatrix very often had people to tea at Hill Top so that they would think she lived there. "She valued her privacy above everything . . ."

Willow Taylor, whose parents kept the *Tower's Arm*, adjacent to Hill Top, says that Beatrix's garden is very much changed. "On the left, as you approached the house, was a vegetable plot, intermingled with flowers, and on the other side a flower bed with lovely old-fashioned flowers, delphiniums, hollyhox, lupins, pansies. A lot of visitors thought it was Peter Rabbit's garden, but it was not. She had not bought Hill Top when she wrote *Peter Rabbit*."

The spirit of Beatrix's remarkable personality lingers inside Hill Top, where the light brings a responsive gleam from oak beams and panelling. Beatrix's life was so closely associated with the house that as you wander round you half expect to come across her, busy at her needlework or thumbing over the certificates she had won at local shows with her farm stock.

Beatrix Potter bought Hill Top with part of the royalties that came from the success of her first book, *The Tale of Peter Rabbit*, plus a legacy from her aunt. Old John Cannon was then in residence, so an end piece was built for he and his family. Beatrix used the old part, as a work place and repository for her treasured possessions. Beatrix and William Heelis lived at Castle Cottage.

When I first knocked on the door of Hill Top over 30 years ago, Mrs. Ted Jackson, the daughter of Tom Storey, gave me a brief glimpse of the rooms and their treasures, apologising for the untidiness and dust. Alterations had been carried out and the workmen not long departed. I came under the gaze of Beatrix Potter as painted by

Hill Top, Sawrey, photographed in 1966. When the centenary of Beatrix Potter's birth occurred in this year there was an upsurge of interest in the authoress (Photo: F. Leonard Jackson).

Delmar Banner, who had posed her with Keswick showfield in the background. At Hill Top, I was shown miniatures of the characters she immortalised and the French dolls with their silken clothes that she loved. Here were photographs, documents and a stylish doll's house. As Squirrel Nutkin collected nuts in the autumn, so Beatrix Potter gathered round herself a stock of quaint but beautiful things. Mrs. Jackson told me that the house became a museum a year after Beatrix Potter died and among the many thousands of visitors who came each year were many from overseas. A grand old Australian lady sat looking at the window ledge for a long time. "Isn't it wonderful," she exclaimed. "They've even kept her vacuum flask." The flask was the one used by Mrs. Susan Ludbrook, the curator. With a sudden influx of visitors, she had had no time to put it out of sight! Mrs. Jackson believed that by writing the books, Beatrix had an outlet after her lonely childhood. The work sprang from her deep love of animals. "She kept guinea pigs, white mice, rabbits and just before her death she had two Pekinese dogs." These were "put to sleep" when Beatrix Potter died.

Tom Storey, who worked for Beatrix Potter for 18 years and served under Mr. Heelis for another two, was in the turnip field on the occasion of my 1955 visit. At the invitation of his son I clambered on to the back of a tractor-drawn trailer. We bumped and jostled up a steep and rocky lane to the field. William Mackereth was Tom's predecessor as the farm man at Hill Top. He worked for Beatrix Potter for 11 years, then retired to Maryport in 1926. Tom arrived at Hill Top after being shepherd for a brief spell at Troutbeck Park. He took over the farm after her death. There are 150 acres of land, the result of a merger of three farms – Hill Top, Castle Farm and Currier Farm. The land, Tom said, is hard and sound. "It can't bide too much dry weather, though."

When Tom and his family moved from Troutbeck Park, they piled their belongings on to a motor lorry kept by Beatrix for the heavy farm jobs. "The garden was nearly a wilderness," Tom told me in one of our many conversations, adding that the district was over-run with rabbits. "It was terrible. Grass couldn't grow. There was hardly any farm stock on the farm." Rabbits also abounded beyond Esthwaite Water, where seventy acres belonged to Beatrix. Jack Hird used to snare these rabbits in October, and in one month he captured 900 rabbits. A wood near Hill Top belonged to the next estate. "That wood was full of rabbits, and they ventured out to graze on Beatrix's land, an area known as The Heights. Willie Heelis and Captain Duke went out with a net, rigged it up near the wood, left the net furled until the rabbits had passed, then slipped the netting down in the hope of capturing rabbits as they sped for cover." It was a good idea which did not have great success in practice. "They were cute, were rabbits, you know," Tom Storey recalled with a smile.

Tom Storey and the farm man had to work especially hard, because Beatrix would not buy any implements. "She didn't try to keep up with the times. Everybody had haytime implements, except us," said Tom. We did, at least, have a mowing machine. Beatrix wouldn't have any alterations to buildings. In the days of John Cannon, she was known to give a hand with the hay. "She'd rake up," I was told.

Hill Top and the adjacent farmer's quarters were inter-connected. "The door went through from our farm kitchen into hers," Said Tom. "My wife used to look after Hill Top in winter and sometimes she'd go through and find Beatrix sitting quietly there, painting. When Hill Top started as a museum, folk kept coming into our house through the connecting door, so it was built up."

An electrical supply arrived in the district, but Beatrix steadfastly refused to have it installed at Hill Top farmhouse. She did permit the shippons to be wired up. "She was the last person in the village to get 'lectric, a year or two after it first came," Tom Storey rcalled. When it came through, she said: 'Well, the cows might like it.' She put electricity into the shippon but the supply went right past the house!" The large dairy at Hill Top "got no sun at all." It was devoted to butter and cheese production. Before the Storeys arrived, Beatrix had a hired dairymaid. Shorthorns were still the most common type of cow, and milking by hand was the rule on most Lakeland farms.

Tom Storey used to "butch" at Hill Top. "She had a licensed slaughter house and at t'back end, she arranged for lambs to be butched and the meat to be taken round the village. Meat was cheap in those days. Lamb cost about sixpence a pound." Tom went round the district "butching" pigs, though Beatrix was not fond of keeping them. She had had a "disappointment" some years before when she attempted to keep pigs. "She had a litter that did not do so well."

When Hill Top was opened as a museum, thousands of visitors arrived. Mrs. Storey had foretold this long before Beatrix died, Tom declared. "One night she said: 'Tell you what it is, father, this place will be a museum one day.' I asked her why she had said that. She said: 'Just go through there and look at the stuff that she's bringing in'. Susan Ludbrook met Beatrix for the first and last time in 1939 and was left with an impression of a person of great delicacy and kindness. Mrs. Ludbrook became the first custodian at Hill Top and in 1966, I persuaded her to recall her Hill Top days for readers of our magazine *Cumbria*. She had been told of the probable opening of the home of Beatrix Potter to the National Trust, and she decided to offer to act as custodian for a short trial season. "The offer was accepted and from the first day I was helped by Freda Storey, the young daughter of the farmer next door, who had always looked after Hill Top for Mrs. Heelis. She loved the old house and I helped her by dusting and polishing furniture. I made the old brass which was such a feature of Hill Top my special responsibility, while Freda, who also loved the garden, and knew Mrs. Heelis's taste in flowers, kept the rooms gay with different blooms as each season came round." Mrs. Ludbrook's special interest lay with the manuscripts and drawings, which Beatrix had left only partly identified, and entirely uncatalogued, though she had inserted slips of paper here and there, indicating her intentions.

"The partnership with Freda Storey lasted the whole of my 13 seasons as custodian, though during that time she married and became Mrs. Jackson, living across the village. The idea of accepting and welcoming strangers to Beatrix Potter's house as visitors was not at all a welcome one to those who had known her shy reticence and dislike of publicity, but Freda gave me every help from the first day and we cared for the old house, and made it live again for those who gladly came from near and far. There was no formal opening, but a number of those interested in the National Trust had gathered by personal invitation, and the house was open to villagers, friends and to any who had known Beatrix Potter and wished to pay tribute to her memory."

The immediate organisation of Hill Top was decided that day. "Visitors would be welcomed and shown round the house and garden and the treasures which Mrs. Heelis collected. No-one knew how many people would seek out the house. Holidays were only just becoming possible again after the austerities of wartime. The Forces were slowly being demobilised and families re-united. Transport was still limited and petrol rationed. Near Sawrey was the comparative isolation, and the retention of the old-world farming atmosphere which had endeared Hill Top to Beatrix Potter, and made it so fitting a background for many of her story-illustrations."

Visitors were enchanted by the wicket-gate, the flagged path, the old stone porch and oak door, the big farm-kitchen and its wide chimney, the old dresser and wide staircase leading to the landing above, the oak bed with flat top on which naughty kittens could play, and best of all the little treasure-room in the middle, with the doll's house, all carefully arranged by Beatrix Potter herself, along with the two fair-haired dolls and their wardrobe. "They fascinated adults and children alike."

Hill Top, Sawrey (Drawn by Edward Jeffrey).

39

Features of Hill Top, Sawrey, in 1970 (Drawn by Edward Jeffrey from photographs taken by W. R. Mitchell).

In 1946, a total of 10,000 visitors was recorded. "The children numbered one in six that first Hill Top season, but the total result and the interest awakened was so satisfactory to The National Trust that it was decided to open at Easter for a full season in 1947, and I was asked to return to resume the custodianship." The great feature of spring, 1947, was publication of Margaret Lane's book, *The Tale of Beatrix Potter*. "She had been at work on it with the consent of Mr. Heelis during his lifetime. It was published in America, too, and immediately became a best seller, doing a great deal to publicise Hill Top and to increase the number of visitors. Visitors in 1947 totalled 5,724 adults and 1,668 children. The result was very satisfactory to The National Trust financially, and reflected the ever-growing interest in Hill Top."

A story of steady progress was recorded. Around 9,000 adults and over 2,000 children visited the house each summer. Any fluctuation in numbers was usually traceable to some local or national source. The old ferry over Windermere had to be taken off and a larger one installed to carry more cars and cope with the increasing traffic on the roads. A steady stream of cars drew up at the village, and took a cup of tea in one of the cottages – in which so many memories of Beatrix Potter lingered – the overall peace and old-world atmosphere was not greatly disturbed. "The rooms in Hill Top are only small, but we could usually cope quite easily in the earlier months of the season, and in September. August was sometimes a problem, and visitors could not always have the immediate attention we aimed to give, but most people were prepared to wait a little while, and enjoy the manuscripts and drawings, and take any opportunities that occurred to ask questions and chat."

Many important and well-known people came as individuals to Hill Top, including some who had a special assignment to carry out. Among these were Margaret Lane, Graham Sutton and Godfrey Winn. H. V. Morton spent a day in the house with a photographer preparing an article for the *National Geographic Magazine*. The "Aunties" from the BBC brought a group of children and gave a broadcast on *Children's Hour*. Freda Jackson was in a radio broadcast with Wilfred Pickles.

In 1951, an unexpected development took place which was to alter the whole future of Hill Top and attract an even wider range of visitors. In May of that year, Leslie Linder paid his first visit, which only lasted three days. "I soon discovered that under his quiet manner and unassuming approach was a specialised interest in the Beatrix Potter stories, and in her art as applied to children's education." Mr Linder wished to compile and publish a book, *The Art of Beatrix Potter*, annotated and made available to students and others interested in this side of her work. "It was not to be a second biography, as this side was admirably covered by Margaret Lane's *The Tale of Beatrix Potter* – which had by this time become the standard work on her life – but a companion book showing Beatrix Potter as an artist, in many more fields than her stories, and throwing light on what had become known as 'the Hidden Years'." Not until the following season, 1952, did Mr. Linder return to Hill Top. He stayed with Mrs. Kenyon, in the corner house across from the *Tower Bank*. This was the village shop around which Beatrix Potter had written her story of *Ginger and Pickles*.

"It was finally decided to print a limited edition of 5,000 copies of *The Art of Beatrix Potter*, so as to preserve for posterity the creative years of one who had stepped unchallenged into her rightful place among Lakeland writers and artists for her purity and clarity of language, and the sheer beauty of her animal portraiture in Lakeland settings. The book, published at four guineas, was quickly sold out. Linder visited Hill Top again in 1957, " and when he saw how often *The Art of Beatrix Potter* was asked for by visitors, and how afraid I was that it might be harmed, he very generously presented another copy to be held in reserve. This I induced him to sign, and it remains in Hill Top." The publication of the book brought an even wider circle of visitors, and the announcement, displayed on the transatlantic liners, that Hill Top was a place of historic interest, caused the number of visitors to rise steadily. So far as possible, each group was met according to any specialised interest shown and accorded individual attention. Susan Ludbrook noticed that the appreciation shown by visitors and the delight expressed by the children was very evident. Many people returned, bringing groups of friends. Some overseas visitors took up National Trust membership for the duration of their stay in England.

In 1959 – the last during which Susan Ludbrook was connected with Hill Top – the sun shone throughout the summer. "Mr. Linder had spent part of his holiday there again, this time bringing his sister." wrote Mrs. Ludbrook. "They both worked on the cataloguing of the manuscripts and were greatly intrigued by one parcel which had never been explored. It turned out to be a bundle of old exercise books with odd leaves interspersed, and one on the top, evidently in German. The whole bundle was tied up with string. On removing the top one, the rest seemed to be in code."

Susan Ludbrook related to readers of *Cumbria* in 1966 what has become a familiar story. "He submitted the code to experts who were skilled in unravelling the usual ones, but the few clues from the Beatrix fragment fitted into no known or accepted sequence, and he began to despair of ever unlocking the secret. Then one Easter evening he decided to have a last try, and to his great surprise and joy found a clue at last within the fragment he had cherished.

"The patient de-coding, magnifying, arranging and assembly of the material into consecutive narrative, which took more than four years of patient, detailed work by an already busy man and his sister, the travelling to Scotland and other places to photograph scenes she described; the visiting of art galleries, and study of newspapers and available documents of the period, have revealed the story of those early hidden years. The publication of it in 1966 was the centenary tribute of Leslie Linder and his sister, Enid, to Beatrix Potter, whom they never knew, but loved through her books and in their personal work among children in Sunday School."

Part of Sawrey (bottom right) and Esthwaite Water (Photo: Aero Pictorial).

The wooden gate at Lakefield, Sawrey, which Beatrix incorporated in one of her paintings.

As Others Saw Her

EVEN IN OLD AGE, Beatrix had a fresh complexion and could at times demonstrate a jolly nature. William Waddington, who lived near her, mentioned her "tight little knitted bonnet" under which was a face that had the complexion of a child's, "with lovely rosy cheeks. She always looked alive and jolly." Tom Storey mentioned her dark brown, rather frizzy hair and the round face, with "a lovely complexion for an old lady." Her clothes were a matter of comment among those who did not know her well. Mrs. Thistlethwaite recalls: "My first memory of her is of seeing her walk down the road wrapped in sacks. She had a bit of a hat on. I thought: 'What a funny old woman.' I suppose I was only about six years old at the time. She just walked down the road, looking at everything, grunting with disapproval at this and that . . ."

When I asked Tom Storey how Beatrix was dressed, he replied: "Not like a lady. She wore the old herringbone costume, the skirt extending down to the ankles, a floppy sort of hat – and clogs on her feet. They were black clogs, with clasps to fasten them." Mrs. Birkett, of Elterwater, recalled the sack Beatrix had worn around her shoulders and an old felt hat that had crowned her head. "I was living at Grasmere at the time I first saw her. I was cook-housekeeper to two old ladies, Misses Mary and Laura Bradley. The thing I remember about Beatrix Heelis is that she was a funny old lady with sack round her shoulders. She wore a trilby hat. A *man's* trilby hat!" Even when being taken for a ride in her chauffeur-driven car, she was not stylishly dressed. "The chauffeur would let her off and just march about till she returned. You would never have thought from what she wore that she was a wealthy person." A lad who was staying with an uncle and aunt at Meadowcroft recalls having to go to Hill Top each morning for the milk. He saw Beatrix, in old clothes, emerging from a pig sty, and he thought: "Poor thing – she has to sleep with the pigs."

Her clogs were made by Charlie Brown, at Hawkshead. He used "kip" or split leather, beech soles and iron caulkers or "irons". Beatrix had rather small feet; she "didn't take above size four." One day, as she walked up Ferry Hill, her clogs clattering on the road, she met a tramp. He looked at her generally shabby appearance and observed: "Times are hard for such as you an' me." When attending Hawkshead Show, Beatrix made an effort to dress well, but her best clothes were old. Mrs. Thistlethwaite says: "You know how a grey tweed goes green with age. Well, this happened with Mrs. Heelis. She didn't care about dress. And she didn't seem to care much for anybody who cared about dress!"

Josephina Banner mentioned her shy nature. She was sometimes thought of as being brusque when she was simply shy. Willow Taylor describes Beatrix as being "a peaceful person and most reserved. She liked solitude. That's why she loved Hill Top. It was tucked away in a quiet spot. Sawrey was really quiet in her day." Beatrix might look like a farmer's wife, but her voice was cultered and refined. There was no trace of a North Country accent. (Charlie Brown was fond of recalling Walter Stevens, her chauffeur, who was a Cockney. He "tried to talk a bit of his own tongue and a bit of the local dialect." Beatrix hired him after he had been serving a local family, and she bought the family car, a Wolseley, to go with him! Walter "drove at about a snail's pace.").

At one time, Beatrix's mother lived at Storrs Park, and when she visited the Castle at Sawrey she travelled in a smart carriage and pair, with a coachman and flunkey. Her mother always reminded William Waddington of Queen Victoria. The Waddingtons would watch the carriage and pair being driven to Beatrix's home, and when it returned Beatrix herself would be sitting in it, wearing her old farming attire which contrasted strongly with the garb of her mother. They would be driven to Bowness in the carriage, and here Beatrix would do her shopping. Mr. Waddington had been told that she would get out of this wonderful carriage and clatter across the causeway into the shops wearing the clogs she had been wearing in the farmyard.

In her latter days, when she was an old lady, she had few real friends. "If she took a fancy to you, everything was alright," said a resident of Sawrey. "She was friendly with farmers. All she seemed to think about towards the latter part of her life was farming. And she didn't know much about it when she came here."

Tom Storey enjoyed his years working for a celebrated landowner. "She was a good person to work for, but she could be 'funny'. You could meet her one time, and she'd never look sideways at you. Another time she would stop and talk. But she never liked to have a long conversation." There were times when she caused offence. Tom related that his wife, having been in bed for a fortnight with internal bleeding, got up and told Tom she would make an effort to feed the hens. "I told her, 'Now don't you go out there. You might not be able to get back.' The hens were on the far side of the field. She went out, though, and Mrs. Heelis saw her feeding the hens. She went out to meet her. She didn't even ask my wife how she felt. She just said: 'Oh, you'll soon get over it. It's nothing.' I thought to myself: 'Now. That's done it. She'll never bother with Mrs. Heelis again.' And she never did. My wife gave her such a telling off that day . . ."

On the other hand, Beatrix was capable of many quiet kindnesses. Tom told me that she was especially fond of old people. Old John Taylor was bedridden. Beatrix visited him regularly. One day she asked him which was his favourite animal, and he replied: "A dormouse." She promptly went home and wrote her book about dormice, which she dedicated to the old man.

What Beatrix acquired she kept. A woman who wished to buy some land at Colwith on which to build a house, wrote to Beatrix who refused, stating that it would spoil the beauty of the area to have a house there. "So we went to Tom Kirby, and managed to buy this place. I wonder what Beatrix would think if she could come back to Colwith now because that spot of ground is a sewage farm!"

Beatrix bought Dale End at Grasmere. When the only son of the farmer was to be married, she gave the old couple notice, stating that they would never be able to manage without their lad. When she arrived at the farm a little while later, the old lady would not let her in. "She shut the door and bolted it."

Tom Storey, who managed Hill Top Farm for Beatrix Potter (A photograph from Tom's own collection).

Top: William Heelis (foreground) with a folk dance group in the early 1930s. Bottom, left: Appleby, from which town came William Heelis (Photo: D. Cassidy). Bottom, right: The premises in Hawkshead where Mr. Heelis, a solicitor, had his office.

Married to Willie Heelis

BEATRIX WAS SHY of people, especially of men, yet when her marriage to William Heelis had taken place in 1913, she walked down the village of Sawrey carrying a plate on which were pieces of wedding cake. The villagers were invited to sample it. "And wish me luck," she added. This story was related to me by William H. Waddington, one of her tenants. In spite of some reluctance on the part of her parents, Beatrix married the quiet, unassuming solicitor who was known to many local people as Appleby Billy, from his origins. The Heelis family had been established at Appleby since 1720, when Thomas had left his native Yorkshire to become land agent to Lord Thanet. Generations of Heelis's served the area as clerics, doctors, land agents or solicitors. Willie had been educated at Sedbergh School. "Broad and tall, he was more like a farmer to look at than a professional man," recalled Clara Boyle. "He had a gentle, understanding smile and a quiet, unruffled voice. He enjoyed a simple life."

On courting nights, as already related, Willie Heelis had arrived at Sawrey with motor bike and sidecar, though it is doubtful if he would ever persuade Beatrix to join him for a ride. "It was a Bradbury motor cycle, which then was *the* bike to have. The sidecar had a superstructure made of wickerwork. We only saw Willie at week-ends. After they were married, she bought him a small car, a Wolseley, but he never made much of his driving. He would drive from Castle Cottage down to the main road, where he had to turn right for Hawkshead. It took him quite a bit of time to get round the corner. We'd hear the gears of the car grating."

Beatrix and Willie had an autumn wedding. The nuptials were at St. Mary Abbot's in Kensington on October 14. It was intended that they should settle at Castle Cottage, but this was in a transitory state as extensions were made. Both Beatrix and Willie had sick relatives. She was attending to her father and he to an old aunt who resided at Appleby. Simultaneously, Warnes in London were requesting Beatrix to supply them with the manuscript and illustrations for another book!

When at home, they helped each other with the housework, even to the extent of sharing with the cooking and curing of hams. Mrs. Thistlethwaite told me of Willie's height, "over six foot." Beatrix called him Willie. "You never saw them together much." In the recollection of Mrs. Richards, he was a very different type from his wife – a tall, gaunt man, "real north country," very happy-go-lucky, fond of business and of pleasure, which included country dancing. "They got on very well in married life; she never interfered with his comings-and-goings." Beatrix never forgot to remind anyone who made a mistake, and called her by her maiden name, of her marital status. "She went round the village with wedding cake and knife on a plate," I was told. She served the cake to villagers and remarked: 'I'm not Beatrix Potter any more; I'm Mrs. Heelis.' "

Mrs. Birkbeck of Great Langdale, described Willie Heelis as a very nice old gentleman. He had his offices at Ambleside. "He was our solicitor when Frank and I built our house. He did all the conveyancing for the land we got, and he always used to ask so kindly after Frank's parents, Jonathan and Mary Jane." Beatrix's solicitor husband was always known in the village as "Appleby Bill," to distinguish him from his partner, who was also Heelis by name. "He was an extremely nice man who did a lot for the farming community," recalled Mr. Waddington. "He even gave helpful advice on Saturdays if the farmers called at his house and asked for it."

Tom Storey told me of evenings that William Heelis spent fishing on a local tarn. "Half of Moss Eccles Tarn belonged to Beatrix. I used to row the boat for him, but she was often there, looking around. We went up to the tarn after his day's work. We used a flat-bottomed boat that is now in the museum at Bowness. It wasn't easy to row, but there wasn't much rowing. You just had to keep it moving! Beatrix had stocked the tarn with brown trout and, by gow, her husband could fish. I've seen him throw a fly a long way and he used to catch a lot of fine trout. He'd give me some, but my family didn't care a big lot for them; they tasted a bit 'mossy'. Beatrix chattered now and again about things she could see up the intake. She was fascinated by sheep and lambs and wanted to know who owned which stock of sheep."

During the 1914-18 war, Willie served on the War Agricultural Committee; he was also a reserve policeman who refused to wear the "tin hat", with which he was issued. Beatrix had long been interested in old customs. When, at Easter, 1912, the "Jolly Boys" (Pace Eggers) went their rounds, she was standing by with camera to record their activity. Beatrix decorated pace eggs and gave them to local children to use in their egg-rolling races on Easter Monday. When after the war, an enthusiasm for folk dancing swept the Lake District, Beatrix was an interested spectator. She did not participate. Willie danced well, and took part. It was said by some people that Beatrix had asked him to join the Sawrey dancing group because she did not want the young girls to be left alone with the male teacher at the time. "She was suspicious of everybody!" Among the contributions that Beatrix made was the provision of attractive dresses for the local folk dancers. Mrs. Thistlethwaite recalls dancing in the large kitchen at Hill Top, Sawrey and adds: "She used to come and watch us dance."

In winter, the dancers gathered in the school at Far Sawrey. Mrs. Thistlethwaite tells that "Mrs. Fyldes, known as "Birdie Fyldes", played the piano." "We danced *Pick up Sticks, Bishop, Comical Fella, If all the World were Paper, Newcastle, Old Mole. . .*" It was a magical time, of summer days with the dancers performing on trim lawns and of

This rowing boat of 1890 belonged to Beatrix Potter. Recovered from the bed of Moss Eccles Tarn in 1976, it is one of many fascinating exhibits at the Bowness Steamboat Museum (Photo: F. Leonard Jackson).

Top, left: Esthwaite Water. Top, right: Clara Boyle, of Ambleside, who shared Mr. Heelis's enthusiasm for folk dancing and organised a number of events in which he and the Sawrey dancers took part. Bottom, left: Hawkshead (Photo: J. Hardman). Bottom, right: Winter sunshine by Esthwaite Water.

winter evenings, in a local hall or, as at Chapel Stile one day, above a local store. The dancers left the room to find it had been snowing heavily. Beatrix recalled another night when they drove home to Sawrey in "frosty starlight." She was to tell of the "mad barbaric music" that attended a performance of the Kirkby Malzeard sword dance at Coniston. In 1929, when Beatrix and Willie attended a folk dancing festival at Underley Hall, near Kirkby Lonsdale, Beatrix drew an imaginative "Dance of the Leaf Fairies" – a drawing that still exists.

Willie Heelis was still greatly devoted to folk dancing when Clara Boyle tried to revive interest in the Ambleside district. "He was approaching the canonical age, and had become somewhat deaf," said Mrs. Boyle, "yet he came regularly to the weekly gatherings I organised at Sawrey and Hawkshead. He was always accompanied by his wife, who never danced a step and did not look as if she could, so stumpy and bent was she by that time. While Mr. Heelis, like the other men, sported his white flannels and open-necked shirt, his wife sat in her rough, dark tweed skirt, pinned up behind with a large safety pin, with a tight-fitting bodice. She always looked out of place on such festive occasions – unless you observed her sweet smile and the loving eyes with which she followed every move of her Willie, lit up with the lamp of comradeship and devotion.

"The great event in Mr. Heelis's career as a folk dancer came in 1930, when the big annual festival gathering took place at Underley Hall, by kind invitation of Lord and Lady Henry Cavendish Bentinck. About 1,000 dancers took part, and there was an equally large number of spectators. "Willie danced his *Newcastle* and *Old Mole* with the best, reflecting credit on the Sawrey team. Then came the great moment, when the three oldest men dancers of the Lake District – Mr. Brady, the 70 year-old little postmaster of Sedgwick, still an ardent rock-climber; Kenneth Spence, of Sawrey House, and Mr. Heelis, danced by themselves the old *Greensleeves* morris jig which, in its buffoonery, demands an appreciable amount of agility, sense or rhythm, and of fun. The three elderly men acquitted themselves with honour, in spite of their having had only one real practice together. Mrs. Heelis was radiant with pride."

Willie was a golfer, also "a terrible big man on the bowling green; he played at Hawkshead," according to Tom Storey. He was also a keen sportsman. "I never saw such a state Hill Top was in when I came down here. It wanted liming; it was over-run with rabbits. Absolutely worried with 'em. A four acre field by t'road was a rabbit warren. One Saturday, Bill Atkinson came to shoot rabbits. I went with him and Mr. Heelis after dinner. At t'roadside field, he put a ferret in a hole and bolted 26 rabbits. Willie Heelis shot 'em all. Didn't miss one. He was a great man wi' a gun. . ." Willie had taken some shooting at Wray. "I were told by some Hawkshead fellas that once he shot two snipe with left and right. They're bad to shoot."

Members of the Postlethwaite family of Sawrey — mother and three children — photographed in the grounds of Lakefield by Beatrix Potter (Photo: Collection of Amanda Thistlethwaite).

Concerning Small Children

DID BEATRIX really like children? After chatting to some of those who knew her at Sawrey, I conclude that most children feared her. Willow Taylor says this was undoubtedly because she was a strange-looking person. She had a habit of chasing children away if they were trespassing. "When you became a teenager, and she could converse with you, she was quite happy in your company. Remember, she was never accustomed to having children about her. In childhood, she had no children as friends."

Mrs. Richards (the former Annie Black) told me she was a girl at school when Beatrix came to live permanently at Sawrey. "I think most children feared her, and she never had any conversation with us. Anyone who appeared unfriendly was someone we regarded as strange, and the best way was to avoid them. It was not often that any of my family came into contact with Beatrix Potter, for we lived well out of the village, but one day my father got a message, asking him to send my brother and me to Hill Top, her home, to receive a book. We must be clean and tidy, making sure of taking a linen bag in which to bring the book home. All the children of school age got the same invitation, and I can tell you there were threats and tears, for we did not want to go. Beatrix Potter received us, and she was kind and pleasant. We were told to take care of the books. Mine was *The Tale of Two Bad Mice*, and my brother's *The Tale of Peter Rabbit*."

If Beatrix Potter scared the children, they did at least get amusement from the sight of the carriage and pair, with its attendant coachman and footman, wearing tall hats and cockades. They were father and son. There was never a smile nor a flick of an eye when they were on duty. This trim outfit belonged to Beatrix Potter's mother, who came to reside near the village. "I remember my father saying: 'There's summat wrong wi't lot of 'em. They don't look quite reight to me.' "

Tom Storey told me: "Local children tended to be frightened of Mrs. Heelis. If they were making a noise – which kiddies do – she would go out and tell them about it, till they got scared of her." Tom used to think she was rather "funny" with children. "I had a little boy and girl when I came down to these parts. She thought the world of the boy, and she didn't like the girl. The reason why she liked the boy was probably because he was very keen on farming, though only four years old." His daughter had asked if she could play in the hayfield. "I said: "yes, but you must play there by yourself; you mustn't let anyone else come with you. By gum, she hadn't been in long when Beatrix landed into t'field. Whether or not she heard kiddies playing, or she'd seen her, I don't know. She ordered her out! Then she went across with a frock skirt of her own for my wife to make her some decent clothes. She thought she should have been dressed like herself, not like any other child, but down to t'ground. She didn't like her playing in the field when the haytime men were there."

The Christmas party for the children of Sawrey is well remembered by Mrs. Thistlethwaite. It was held at Castle Cottage on a Saturday afternoon, from 3 p.m. until 6 p.m. "She used to open up her sitting room. She had all the things taken to other parts of the house and we always started with tea, then a dance. Tea was served in a big room upstairs, after which we'd come downstairs and dance, with Mr. Heelis playing the pianola. He always started with a folk dance, *Roger de Coverley*. We children were aged from about five to 10. There'd be 30 of us. Mrs. Heelis dressed herself up in her black satin and she was the life and soul of the party. We had Christmas cake, jelly and other party food." The repast was prepared by the ever-faithful Mrs. Rogerson. Beatrix once took Amanda into a small room and showed her a book she had written. "You know what children are like. I was perhaps hoping she would give that book to me." recalls Mrs. Thistlethwaite. She did give me it in the end. Its the only thing I was ever given, except my wedding present – a cheque for £2. I should have kept that cheque, shouldn't I?"

After telling me about the parties for children, Mrs. Thistlethwaite observed: "As she got older, she got rather bitter against children. I feel it was because times had altered. Children were now more 'forward', and she couldn't abide that." Willow Taylor said: "If she saw me in one of her fields, she would go straight to my mother and I was in great trouble. I was something of a 'tom boy' when I was a child. Father would say: 'How many times have I told you to keep off Mrs. Heelis's land?' " Mrs. Taylor added: "When we were small, we knew her as Mrs. Heelis, not as Beatrix Potter. We didn't think of her as being a famous authoress. We knew she wrote little books, but we never visualised her as being a great person. She didn't like publicity. She didn't seek fame at all."

Edna Benson, reared at Troutbeck Park, remembers "a little old lady wearing a black shawl." Adding that "we children were more interested in the chauffeur, Old Walter. He had a pocketful of sweets for us!" Every year, Edna received a book from Beatrix. "She used to come to Troutbeck Park quite often and just before Christmas one year she said to my mam: 'What have you bought Edna for Christmas?' Mam said: 'I've bought her a twin-set.' 'What colour?' 'Red.' 'Oh, Mrs. Benson, you must take it back to the shop. If your little girl is out where there are some bullocks, they'll chase her.' My Mam had to take that twin-set back to the shop and she got me a blue one." Anthony Benson believes that she did good in many unpublicised ways. "In her time many people were poor. The farthest thought in their heads would be to have owt much for dinner. . . Many a time, such as on a Sunday, Beatrix would bob 'em a joint o'meat."

Did Beatrix truly dislike children? One suspects that it was the modern child, "pampered and spoilt", she did not care to meet. Children who knew their places and were not cheeky, were treated well. And, after all, *The Tale of Benjamin Bunny*, one of her best books, was dedicated thus:

FOR THE CHILDREN OF SAWREY

from

OLD MR. BUNNY

A Beatrix Potter character from the Royal Doulton Museum collection. This subject, Ginger, is no longer in production (Photo: Royal Doulton, Limited).

Objects owned by Beatrix Potter. She was an avid collector of bric a brac (Photography by permission of the National Trust).

Among the varied objects owned by Beatrix Potter was a stuffed pine marten in a case, teapots, mugs and a substantial oak chair (Photography by permission of the National Trust).

Top: A view from the window of the room at Troutbeck Park farmhouse which Beatrix Potter used when visiting her property here. Bottom: An old painting of the Troutbeck Park estate (Photography by permission of The National Trust).

Off to Troutbeck!

AFTER HER MARRIAGE, Beatrix enjoyed the real country life. To be out and about, walking across the good earth, watching cattle being fed or milked, seeing the sheep being gathered for clipping, gave her much pleasure. In the 1914-18 war, concerned that the Army might suddenly demand the farm horses, she observed that "at a pinch we can use cattle"! One ploughing time, the ploughman was called up for military service and other arrangements must be hurriedly made. Beatrix owned cows, sheep, horses, poultry and pigs. She was very fond of pigs, and especially a pet, Sally, who followed her round the village, responding whenever Beatrix called her name.

In 1923, she became the owner of one of Lakeland's largest sheep farms – Troutbeck Park, at the head of its own little valley, flanked by the lean ridges of the fells that have gathered around High Street. She visited Troutbeck Park regularly and maintained a small room here as a place into which she might withdraw. The isolated farmhouse, visible from the road between Windermere and Kirkstone Pass is substantial and white-washed, as is the local custom. Behind it rises The Tongue (from an Old Norse word meaning "a ridge between two valleys that join"). Buzzards circle and mew. Red deer occupy some of the local fells. Ravens call with their gruff voices then flick on their backs during flight, as though for the sheer joy of living. On the fells are Herdwick sheep. Beatrix improved the local stock with the help of such specialists as Anthony Benson and Tom Storey.

Tom was persuaded to go to Troutbeck Park as he pondered on the necessity to leave the employ of Noble Gregg, who farmed in the village. He had worked for him for a dozen happy years. Beatrix heard about Tom's impending move and she sought him out, arriving – unannounced – as Tom completed the hand-milking of a dozen Shorthorn cows. It was at 6 p.m. on a November Saturday in 1926. Beatrix is recalled as "a little woman, and bonnie-looking."

She asked his name. "I told her."

"She said: 'Well, I'm Mrs. Heelis. I hear you're leaving Mr. Gregg's farm.' I said: 'Yes'. She said: 'Will you come and work for me?' I said: 'Yes, I don't mind – if the money's right.'

"She asked: 'How old are you?' I said: 'I'm thirty.' 'Oh,' she said, 'I'm sixty.' Just like that. She asked me how much I was getting as a wage. She was quite straight about it. I told her. 'Well,' she said, 'if you work for me I'll double it.' I said it was all right.

"She asked me when I could start. I said I would start on Monday. I'd nowhere else to go, and I was married then. That was how it happened. I went to Troutbeck Park on the following Monday. . ."

I asked Tom to furnish more information about the visit to Town End of the celebrated authoress. In the shippon, on that November evening, a dozen Shorthorns were quietly dining on hay. "At five o'clock we cleaned them out; made their tubs, milked them, then 'fothered' them for the night." Noble Gregg was known as a speedy milker, "and I wasn't bad miself." It took just over five minutes to milk a cow. "We reckoned that one man could milk a dozen cows, if they were good to do, in an hour."

What prompted her to seek out Tom at Troutbeck? "I didn't find out till quite a long time after. Tommy Atkinson and his brother lived at the next farm to Hill Top. They had tried showing Herdwick sheep. They gave over because they couldn't make anything of it. Mrs. Heelis had bought one or two of these sheep off them; she didn't want them to be sold and taken out of the district. News spread that I was leaving Town End. Mrs. Heelis – who was wanting a man to look after her sheep – went round the district 'getting my character'. I heard that a while after! She went to the old farmers in the district who knew me, asking them what sort of a man I was." She had been driven to Town End in a brand-new, bull-nosed Morris Cowley, by Tommy Christie, who was the forester on the estate and "doubled up" as chauffeur. Tommy lived at Colthouse.

Tom Storey, in 1926, was married, with two young children. He and his family lived at a cottage in the village. He was looking forward to living at Troutbeck Park, but before he had an opportunity of moving in, Mrs. Heelis asked him to take over at Hill Top, Sawrey. "She wanted to show Herdwick Sheep. Why she couldn't show them from Troutbeck Park I don't know, because there were about 1,000 Herdwick ewes there." She had no sheep but Herdwicks, and called other breeds 'mongrels'! When Tom said that he would prefer to go to Troutbeck Park, she offered to augment his wage if he would manage the Sawrey farm instead. "I said: 'All right. If wife's willing, then I'm willing to move to Sawrey. That's how we landed. . ."

When Beatrix had bought Troutbeck Park, "she thought that Englishmen were no good among sheep, so she employed a Scotsman at the farm. Her brother farmed in Scotland, you see. She got to know all about the Scottish ways, which were different to those we followed down here. She wanted the Scottish routine at Troutbeck Park, but folk laughed at her. And she learned her lesson."

Tom was at Troutbeck Park for 12 months. "I put rams on to a thousand breeding ewes and I lambed them the following spring. It had been 'tipping time' when I went, being November. I marked 992 lambs out, and some didn't mark out; I left them for the fox. You marked as many as you thought fit, and you forgot two or three that were left to lamb, because foxes would go with them." The mark for Troutbeck Park was a red on

Two views of Troutbeck — the village and some of the flanking hills. Beatrix Potter purchased Troutbeck Park, the old sheep farm at the head of the valley (Photo: T. Parker).

The spire of St. Mary's rises above the rooftops of Ambleside (Photo: F. Leonard Jackson).

the "hook" (where the thigh bone sticks up). "They hadn't had very good luck with lambing at Troutbeck Park because it was a devil of a farm for sheep fluke. There'd been no cure for it in those days. When I went to Troutbeck Park, the cure came from a veterinary firm at Newcastle.' By jove, we used it that back end, and it was life-saver, we got it in the form of capsules."

Anthony Benson first worked at Troutbeck Farm as a lad fresh from school – the farm was then owned by Mrs. Leach – and after a year he moved away. He had a variety of jobs. When he was working for Isaac Fleming, he heard from Mr. Heelis, who was Isaac's solicitor, that a shepherd was needed at Troutbeck Park. "I know a bit aboot that spot," said Anthony. Mr. Heelis asked: "Would it be any good sending Mrs. Heelis up to see you about it?" Anthony said: "Aye. There's no harm." In due course, Beatrix arrived. Anthony inquired how much wage he would receive. He had been earning 25 s. "Mrs. Heelis offered me £4.10s straight off. She built us a cottage. She kept us in coal. She fed the dogs. (I always used to keep five or six dogs). With all the extras, that wage was as good as £6."

Anthony's wife, Sarah, was a "townie", from Workington. ("She was at the post office at Borrowdale when I first met her.") Mrs. Heelis got on well with her. "One day, she asked me if I had a bank book. I said: 'I don't know what sort of a thing that is.' She told me about it and said that if I started a bank account, for every £1 I put in she'd add £1. It went on for 15 years." Anthony showed her the bank book when she came to pay him every fortnight. She saw to it that whatever he had put in the account was doubled.

They had their differences, of course. One day, Beatrix and Anthony differed in their assessment of how a farm job should be done. "Watter used to run down one side of a fence. She wanted watter to come underneath that fence. She took me to it and showed me what had to be done. I said: 'That's wrong, Mrs. Heelis.' She said: 'who's payin' for the job, Benson?' Well we just had to git on with it. She came back later. 'What do you think about the job now, Benson? I said: 'It's still all wrong.' Said Beatrix: 'Well, do it your own way.' " And she stomped off.

Beatrix was most happy walking with the springy turf underfoot and the mountain breeze in her face. "She was a lish body," recalls Anthony. "She would walk around the fields where there was a lot of sheep. Or she'd set off on a hill track." She found sheep clipping time, with its noise and bustle, most exhilarating. "We clipped between 2,000 and 3,000 sheep – all Herdwicks. It took about seven hours simply to 'gather'. The sheep went as far as High Street and round by Caud'l. Before her day, there had been a boon clip, with neighbours helping. It was always on the last Tuesday in June." Some local people sighed for the lost glories of the "boon clip". A meal had been served in the barn. "There were trestle tables. The main course was beef, new tatties and Yorkshire pudding." At night, when work was done, more refreshments were served and the day ended with dancing. "Under Mrs. Heelis, we just clipped away by ourselves. I've seen us sit down of a morning at 7 o'clock, and clip, then git up and have our dinners, and back and sit down again, and clip till 6 o'clock. It went on maybe for a fortnight or three weeks. There were always four of us clipping. I was the shepherd, so many a day I didn't get sat down. I was away fetchin' some more sheep in. We fed well, but there was no 'do' afterwards."

At Troutbeck Park, Galloway cattle were reared for beef. "We had only one milk cow, for household use. If that cow ran dry, they took it down to Hill Top and fetched another. We'd always plenty o' milk." The Galloways were of good quality, from stock bought at Newcastleton, on the Borders. "I'd nowt to do with the cows," said Anthony. "My job was sheep. I never went wi' them when they were buying or selling cows. They used to take calves from Troutbeck to Newcastleton by motor wagon, and stay overnight. Mrs. Heelis would go to t'bull sale." After a serious illness in the late 1930s, her recuperation was assisted by visits to her beloved Troutbeck Park, where she watched the Herdwick sheep being clipped and saw her fine beef cattle. There were 30 beasts, with calves at foot, and a white bull. She also attended Keswick Tup Fair. "She wore the same old costume, day in and day out. It was a thick tweed and reet doon to her ankles." Anthony never saw her judging sheep. "I've seen her looking at 'em. She didn't know a gurt lot about sheep. She was a body who took a lot o' notice of such as Old Isaac Thompson, Ned Nelson and all them old flockmasters."

Anthony was one of those indomitable men who, in October, drove young sheep long distances from fell farms such as Troutbeck Park to winter grazings in lower land – an area that was overswept by mild breezes from the sea. "We used to take sheep, mainly shearlings, to Home Fell at Coniston and Tarn Hows. The hoggs (last year's lambs) went on to Birker Moor. We set off from Troutbeck Park as soon as it came daylight and took maybe 600 sheep altogether, in two trips. Two of us with two or three dogs, drove sheep down to Lowwood and on to Waterhead, then ower Rothay Brigg, up to Skelwith Brigg and over top of Oxen Fell to Coniston. They just had a few sheep at Sawrey. Birker Moor was the farthest we went. I've put some queer days in there."

In April, the Birker Moor sheep were walked to Tilberthwaite where "we'd stop aw neet. Lile Tommy Stoddart was at Tilberthwaite then and he used to put us up overneet and help us next morning to come through by t'quarries to top of Oxen Fell. . . If you were on t'road wi' t'sheep Mrs. Heelis passed you three or four times to see that all was going well. If there was a lame dog, she'd pick it up, take it home and fetch you another dog. Mind you, if *you* were lame, she wouldn't! She watched the droving operation from her car, which was driven by the implacable Walter Stevens, "a grand auld fella."

At lambing time, Joe Mosscrop, a special "doctor" was accommodated at Troutbeck Park. He was from Scotland. "Mrs. Heelis thought the world o' that man. He came every year I was there to look after the waifs and strays." Joe was a good sheep doctor. "He had a drop o' gin in a bottle, and he used to put two or three drops on to a lamb's tongue to warm it up. I've seen us working at dark o' neet, wi' just an oil lamp. (We'd no electricity then)." Joe, an elderly man, was "a wiry old customer". His dog, Jess, was first-rate. Anthony tried to buy it off him. Several times he asked and several times he was refused. "It got to five pund, which was a big price then. I said: 'I'll gie thee five pun', Joe, for that dog. Just leave her. If she settles down, it'll be O.K. If she doesn't, she'll be here next time you come back. I wanted it because it had a gey lot o' eye, and it was just the job for working on a fell top." Anthony relates that Joe would go into the field with Jess and say: "Catch me this, Jessie, please." He always said please when addressing the dog! (It used to make the other men laugh.) The dog would enter the field and grab the desired sheep by the cheek, "but it wadn't mark it."

Beatrix had an old dog called Bob. "It was a lile bow-legged thing, though he'd been a good dog in his time. When I first went to Troutbeck Park, Mrs. Heelis had four or five dogs of her own. I used to think that Bob was a useless old thing. But you had to take it with you." There was one day when Anthony and Bob reached an area on the fell where there was a sheep trod. "Bob wouldn't gang any further. It went on that trod that day and was never seen again. . . We wasted many a day looking for it. Mrs. Heelis came up every day to help." Six or seven old dogs that had been pensioned off had a special kennel which she inspected whenever she visited Troutbeck Park. "The kennel had to be cleaned out properly."

When Anthony killed a badger, he thought he had done a good thing. Mrs. Heelis got to know about it and she asked why he had slain the badger. "I said: 'Well a badger worries lambs and things like that.' She said: 'Oh, no it doesn't.' I nearly got my notice over that badger. She was reet upset." Beatrix disliked foxhunting, and she would not have the hunt on her land, but she agreed to "summer" a hound for the local pack. Anthony told me: "If there was a hunt not so far from Troutbeck Park in winter, I was missing!"

Tom Storey's brief sojourn at Troutbeck Park – he left in June, 1925, to manage Hill Top at Sawrey – was a happy one. "Troutbeck Park was her pet farm. She used to visit the place regularly. She'd take a sandwich with her and go for a walk on to the fell." She did not often enter the farmhouse. "She just left her car in the yard and away she'd go through t'fold. If I happened to be away up t'fell, she'd go to Tongue End and wait for me coming back. She carried a stick, not a crook, with her." Tom would come down off the fell, sit with her for a while and report whatever had happened. "It was not often she could be persuaded to come into the farm kitchen for a drink o'tea. She just had her sandwiches, which were lapped in a piece of paper. She ate 'em outside."

THE TALE OF
LITTLE PIG ROBINSON

from Mrs Heelis
Christmas 1929

Boat landings near The Ferry Hotel, on the west shore of Windermere, in Victorian days (From the album of the Gaddum family, courtesy of Brockhole).

Above: Castle Cottage, Sawrey, the home of Beatrix Potter. Below: One of her Lakeland farms at Tilberthwaite which she purchased with the Monk Coniston estate.

Top: Tom Storey and his son with a prize-winning Herdwick belonging to Beatrix Potter (Photo: Tom's own collection). Bottom, left: Beatrix Potter in later life, at Eskdale Show, painted by Delmar Banner (Courtesy of Abbot Hall, Kendal). Bottom, right: A cup awarded to Beatrix for sheep exhibits at a Lakeland show (Tom Storey collection).

In Love with Herdwicks

THE HERDWICK is Lakeland's own little breed of sheep, being well suited to life on the craggy mountains. A Herdwick thrives where many another breed of sheep would die. One story tells how the first sheep of this breed to be seen in Lakeland were washed ashore from a galleon of the Spanish Armada wrecked on the Cumbrian coast near St. Bees; another tale relates that sheep of this type were brought to the region by the Norsemen. A third account is that Herdwicks are simply the descendants of a tough indigenous breed that had adapted itself to severe local conditions. The wool of the Herdwick may be poor but, say the Lakeland flockmasters, the mutton is "the mutton of kings".

Beatrix's enthusiasm for Herdwicks was developed through a family friendship with Canon Rawnsley, founder of the Herdwick Sheepbreeders' Association. He wrote romantically about the Herdwick, as the following passage indicates. "The shepherd knows that a lamb suckled on its native 'heaf' or pasturage will never forget it, and though it be taken by force from the hills, if it have only been mothered there for fourteen days, it will drink in such a homing instinct with its mother's milk, as will guide it back over hill and dale to the pasturage of its infancy... Very interesting it is to watch the shepherds take them to the fell. They do not open a gate and let them scatter where they will, rather... they take them to the furthest part of the pasture they are to range, furthest that is from the farm in the valley, and there leave them. Instinctively the flock know its utmost limit, and will begin to feed backwards towards the dale."

Tom Storey told me: "Beatrix thought a lot about the Herdwick sheep; she wasn't particularly interested in farming in general. She didn't knaw one cow from another..." Her finest moment was when one of her Herdwicks was awarded a trophy at a Lakeland show. Tom, who she employed especially to improve her sheep stock, said she was driven to the shows by her husband, the uncomplaining Willie, in his little Ford car. The first trophy to be won for Mrs. Heelis was awarded to one of her shearlings at Hawkshead in 1928; two years later, her sheep claimed any number of major prizes at the shows, and Tom received a cup marked Ennerdale, Loweswater, Eskdale, 1930, "for champion female." The cup was made for Mrs. Heelis who, of course, retained the original trophy. Mrs. Heelis kept the cups; Tom was allowed to retain teapots and tankards. Tom and others were wryly amused at a show, when Beatrix didn't "ken" her own sheep. At Keswick Show, where she was photographed with Lady Leconfield, she later talked her way to the sheep pens. "All the old sheep farmers knew her. She'd talk for a week to a real old sheep farmer. I was standing there talking to two men; we were leaning on the pens, and straight across were our sheep. She walked down the side of the pens with old Mr. Mackereth, who was a hind before I came to Hill Top. As it happened, I was showing one sheep that she should have known. It was one of t'elder sheep, a ewe. I saw them walking near the pens, then stop suddenly, and she talked about sheep. Then she whipped round and said: 'Which is such-and-such ewe, Storey, among these?' I said: 'Them aren't yours! Yours are in next pen.' Was her face red! I don't think she liked it but she daren't say anything. I was only telling the truth."

Tom told me of her favourite outfit, which was made of Herdwick tweed. "Once she gave me three fleeces from our show ewes and I had a suit made up from the wool. That suit was cut in the late 'thirties'. It's rough tweed – but it still wears well!"

Josephina Banner first met Beatrix at Eskdale Show, a celebrated event for the Herdwick men of the western dales. It so happened that on this occasion, Beatrix was among the judges. Majestic Herdwicks, daubed with "show red", their faces coarse and white like hoar-frost, were paraded before the diminutive lady, who was suitably attired in her tweedy outfit, with clogs on her feet and a felt hat held in place with elastic under the chin, to cheat any Cumbrian breezes. Josephina, and her husband Delmar, were introduced to Beatrix by Cyril and Sally Bulman, who had come to help their relations at the *Woolpack* inn, Boot. "As a sculptor, I was wearing my usual working attire – boiler suit – and had clogs on my feet. I think she liked me instantly because of the clogs. We got on with each other because we were both straightforward people."

The Banners watched her judging the stock. Then they saw her wander around the sheep section of the show, looking intently at animals in the pens. "You could see that the farmers respected her." Then a big, tall farmer approached her – and slapped her on the back, as he might have done with a well-built farmer friend. "The blow was so hard it nearly toppled her over, and she staggered. He had drunk too much and was just too friendly. He told her that his ancestors had known John Peel, the famous huntsman. Sometimes, when Peel was really drunk, one of the family had lifted him on to his horse. Beatrix was determined not to be impressed. She simply said: 'I've never thought anything of John Peel.' It was a brave thing to say in front of all those farmers, because they all thought that John Peel was marvellous."

When Mr. C. T. Williamson was a young shepherd in his teens, he was on Eskdale showfield with some Herdwick sheep, making them ready for the show ring. Mr. Williamson recalls: "After two days walking over the tops by Wasdale Head, plus a real wet Lakeland morning, the sheep were not looking their best. Coming towards me was an odd sight – Mrs. Heelis, with a hessian bag around her waist and another folded mid-bottom which covered her head and shoulders; she was definitely waterproof.

"Assisted by her shepherd, she was putting the final touches to her Herdwick sheep.

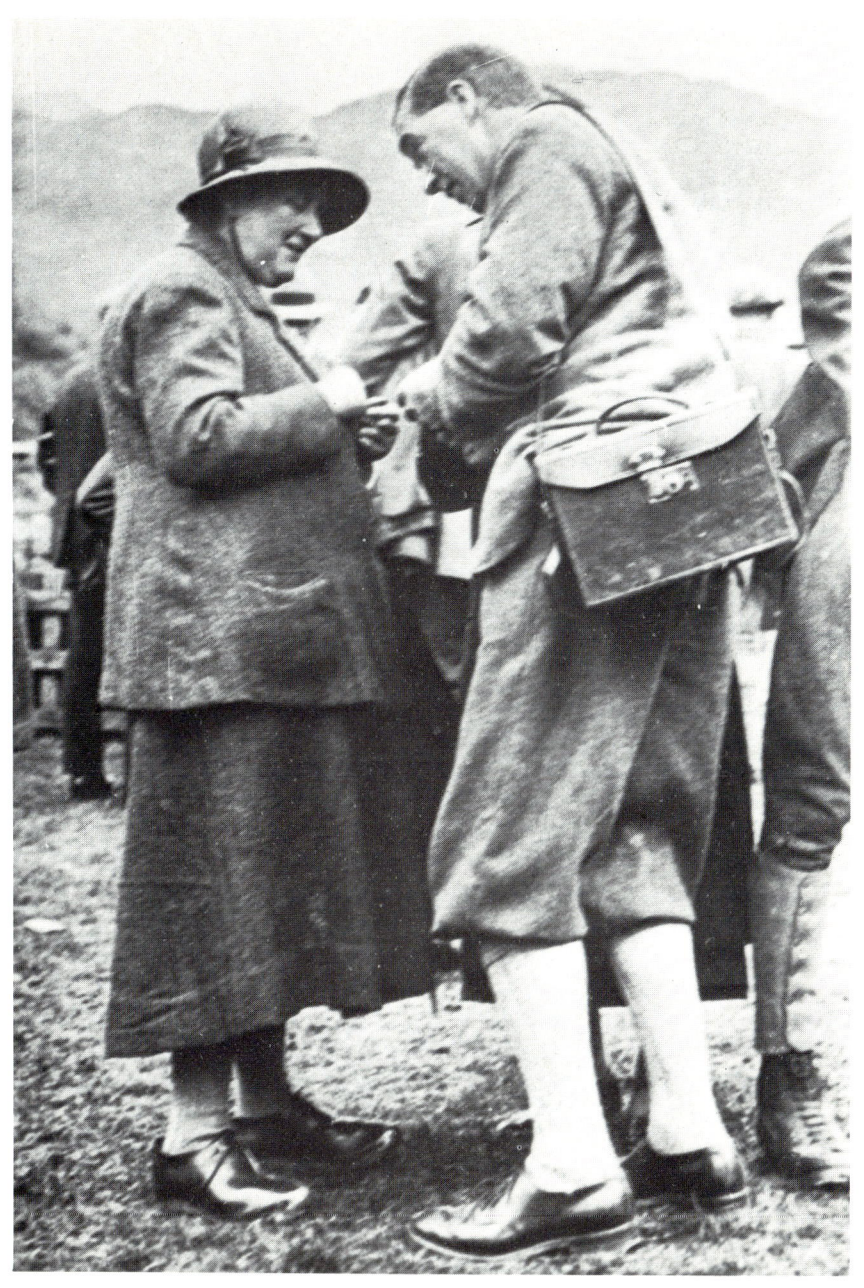

Beatrix Potter, in homely tweeds, with visitors to Eskdale Show (Photo: Victoria and Albert Museum).

**Herdwick Billy, one of the Lakeland flockmasters Beatrix met at Eskdale
Show (Photo: J. Hardman).**

These would later be judged by two appointed shepherds along with many more entries. I was amazed by the manner she went about her job. She was really enjoying it, despite the rain. She knew her beloved Herdwicks and would argue with anyone on their merits. When I hear her name, either mentioned or in print, my thoughts go back to that Eskdale Show incident. She was an odd lady, but was at home with her sheep."

A Herdwick tup.

Delmar and Josephina Banner were at the *Woolpack* Eskdale, when they met a professor of agriculture at Durham, who mentioned the circumstances in which he came to meet Beatrix. He had sent a questionaire round the district, seeking information about sheep diseases. One of the most helpful replies came from a farmer called B. H. Heelis. He made an appointment to see this farmer, and in due course he arrived at the Cottage at Sawrey, where "their little maid" took him upstairs to a tiny room. In an enormous bed was this tiny, pretty old lady – B. H. Heelis, the farmer. He had tea with her and was enchanted by what she told him about sheep diseases.

Anthony Benson recalls that on the showfield, all the old flockmasters used to go and talk to her. "There was Herdwick Billy and Isaac Thompson, who used to be at West End, Wythburn, and Edward (Ned) Nelson o' Gatesgarth. All them auld fellas liked to meet her and she enjoyed talkin' to 'em." Beatrix "was one of those who'd take a fancy to one sheep when there were mebbe plenty better 'uns." She liked Herdwick sheep, "and you hadn't got to keep any of t'others. On a fell spot like Troutbeck Park, it was not always easy to keep the flock pure Herdwick with stray tups coming in from other places."

Anthony's mind is a repository of old-time sheep lore. "At places like Keswick, you used to hire a tup. It might cost £1, £2 or £3 – if it was a good 'un, mebbe more. You used that tup and had to winter it till May, when you took it to the spring show and returned it to its owner, paying him for being able to use it." The tups wore "show red", their fleeces being smeared with red rudd. Anthony describes their showtime condition as "weshed up an' ivverything." In due course, the old hiring custom began to give way to outright sales. There was a keen demand for the best tups. "If Mrs. Heelis wanted one, she would have it. She once paid nearly £200 for a tup, and £200 was a lot of money in those days."

You'd see her at many of the fell shows – at Ennerdale, Loweswater, Gosforth and Eshd'l (Eskdale). Tom Storey recalled when he and the helpers were out of their beds at 5 a.m. on show day. "I milked 12 cows then. The show sheep were kept in a handy pasture and we had a little lorry to transport 'em. Tommy Christopherson drove the lorry. We took a shearling and a hogg, two tups, a two-shear tup, two ewes, two two-shears, four twinters and two lambs. Mrs. Heelis never saw the sheep till the time I brought them into the farmyard, just before a show, and put the 'show red' on 'em. You had to be particular about putting on 'show red'. You could get too much on and then it'd spoil the look of 'em. I used to wash their faces and their legs with soap and water. I did it again when I'd got them in the pen at the show ground." Tom's sheep were ready for showing at 10 a.m. "Then Mrs. Heelis would turn up, in a car, and make over towards them. She'd look the sheep over and talk to t'auld farmers about 'em."

Tom added: "Folk thought yon sheep got fed, but they didn't. I proved that with Jimmy from Knott Houses at Grasmere. He came down one Sunday with Teddy Tyson, who used to show a lot. We'd looked at t'show sheep, which were down t'bottom meadow. Jimmy said: 'I don't see any troughs in that field.' I said: 'No, thou wean't;

them sheep don't get any feed i' summer. Nobbut in winter.' 'Oh,' he said, 'I always feed my show sheep through summer.' I said: 'I don't. I think they last longer if they don't get too much feed.' "

One might expound at length on how much Beatrix knew about sheep farming. She did ensure the continuation of the pure breed of Herdwick in its true home on the central mountains and on the dalehead farms. She was elected the first woman President of the Herdwick Sheepbreeders' Association. As long ago as 1903, she sketched the distinctive sheep marks of the area around Fawe Park, Keswick, where she was holiday making with her family. She wrote movingly of the demise at Hill Top of an outstanding Herdwick ram, "a grand old champion of the fells. . ." This was Josiah Cockbain's *Saddleback Wedgewood*, which was "the perfect type of hard, big-boned, Herdwick tup, with strong clean legs, springy fetlocks, broad scope, fine horns, a grand jacket and mane. He had strength without coarseness. A noble animal."

Lakeland shepherd at Lambing Time (Photo: J. Hardman).

This tree near Lakefield, Sawrey, was the subject of a water-colour sketch
by Beatrix Potter. Below: An outbuilding at Lakefield.

Top: A prospect of Coniston Water from the Monk Coniston estate.
Below: The big house at Monk Coniston in daffodil time.

This photograph, of Beatrix Potter in her later days, also shows Tom Storey. The photograph was taken by R. S. Hart, who stayed with Mary Fleming. Mary (nee Postlethwaite) was mentioned in Beatrix's journal (Photo: Collection of Mary's sister, Amanda. The picture has been greatly enlarged).

The Last Days

JOSEPHINA BANNER says: "Beatrix was tiny, and the older she got, the tinier she became. She was so cute and pretty – the prettiest old lady I have ever met. The eyes were of a brilliant blue. She had lovely, rosy cheeks and pretty white hair, done up with a little black velvet bow." When they last met it was a garden occasion. They walked beside the flower garden, then near the apple trees, then in the vegetable plot to a strip of ground which housed local wildflowers, she had collected and planted. Among them was "zig-zag clover", Beatrix's name for a variety of plant associated with Timmy Willie, who waved it to Tommy Town Mouse in one of the famous tales.

Beatrix and Josephina walked to the little iron gate set between mossy posts. "She pulled my head down to her level and she kissed me. Neither of us spoke. We knew, as we parted company, that we would never meet again. When I turned round, there was Beatrix, waving a clover leaf at me. Just like Timmy Willie."

Beatrix died in 1943, aged 77. A few hours before her death, Tom Storey was at her bedside. "Mrs. Rogerson told me she wanted to see me. Would I come across after I'd finished the farm work? I said: 'Aye, I'll be across.' Tom hand-milked the Shorthorn cows – there were no milking units at Hill Top as long as Beatrix was alive – and he finished about six o'clock. "Then I went into the house, and had a wesh and a bite to eat – what we called supper. I didn't change all through, but just put a decent jacket on."

Mrs. Rogerson admitted him to Castle Cottage. Willie Heelis was not at home. Beatrix lay in bed "at yon end of t'house". There was no fire in the room. "I sat down and we chatted about farming. She asked how things were going on. I think she thought she was 'going' the way she talked to me that night. One thing she asked me to do – and I thought it was the main thing she asked me to come across for – was to carry on looking after the farm for Mr. Heelis after her day. (I'd had a letter asking me to do the same thing. It had been written in pencil when she was lying in hospital in Manchester two years before she died). I left her about seven o'clock. I hadn't stayed long. She died during the night."

On Christmas day – "at dinnertime" – Willie Heelis arrived at Hill Top with her ashes. "She'd told me where she wanted 'em putting – nobody else knows." Willie brought 'em into the kitchen wrapped in newspaper. He said: "You'll know where these have to go, Storey."

Willow Taylor recalls: "When Mrs. Heelis died, it was a sad day for the whole village. "The weather just before Christmas that year was cold and miserable. The war was running its uneasy course. It was a time of austerity, with ration books needed for basic necessities. At night, no artificial lights were visible outdoors. There was just the cold light from the moon – and a glare from Barrow-in-Furness on the days when bombs were dropped. The people of Sawrey shared with many other communities the dread of hearing the distinctive wavering drone of enemy aircraft, some of which jettisoned spare

Beatrix Potter, in her old age, with Alison Hart, the daughter of R. S. Hart. The Pekingese was the last dog to be owned by Beatrix (Photograph, taken c1943, was given to Mary Fleming and is now in the possession of her sister Amanda).

bombs' at the start of the homeward run. The Home Guard maintained a presence at Sawrey. German Prisoners-of-war were quartered at the nearby Grizedale Hall.

Tom Storey finished his Christmas dinner, had his usual "sit-down" and then went for a walk with the parcel that Willie Heelis had brought. "It was a bonny day," he recalled. He reverently scattered Beatrix's ashes on the Hill Top high pastures.

In its obituary, *The Times* noted that Beatrix Potter had died in the days just before Christmas, "a time at which, for the last 40 years, she had been much in the minds of happy children. It is no mean epitaph, and they are legion who think of her gratefully." Delmar Banner, in an appreciation that appeared in *The Times* on December 30, noted: "Her many farm tenants all over the dales honoured her as a landlord of care and understanding. She was a noted breeder and judge of Herdwick sheep. At all sheep shows could be seen her short, stout, venerable figure, her countenance full of intelligence and humour, her plump, apple-rosy cheeks, and shrewd blue eyes. She was a Cumbrian, solid, realistic, truthful."

To the writer in the *New York Herald Tribune* (issue of January 6, 1944), Beatrix was a "North-Country farmer, connoisseur of old furniture and china, lover of nature and animals. . . an artist both with words and with brush." Her greatness lay in the fact that she was able again and again to create that rare thing – "a book that brings grown-ups and children together in a shared delight."

In her will, Beatrix bequeathed nearly all her possessions to Willie during his lifetime. Sums of money were left to two cousins. Frederick Warne Stephens received her shares in the publishing firm of Frederick Warne; on the death of Willie he would also acquire the rights and royalties in her books. Remembered in her will were personal friends and helpers, including Tom Storey and her chauffeur Walter Stevens. She instructed that a meadow at Satter Howe, on Ferry Hill, should be kept in memory of local men who perished in the 1914-18 war.

There remained her greatest legacy – some 4,000 acres of property, including 15 outstanding farms – to The National Trust, which had been established largely through the efforts of her good friend Canon Rawnsley. She specified that the rooms at Hill Top, Sawrey, should be kept as she had left them. The house was not to be tenanted. The sheep on her fell farms should continue to be pure Herdwick, and there must be no hunting by otter hounds and harriers at Troutbeck Park.

Willie Heelis was in a sad physical state at the time his wife died. "He had prostrate gland trouble. He wouldn't go away to be operated on," Tom Storey related. "In the end, they had to take him away." He was moved to Purey Cust nursing home at York. Tom went to see him just before he died, in 1945. "I could tell he was a long way on. . ."

Overleaf: Photograph courtesy of Royal Doulton, Limited.